W9-BMG-115

The Wisdom of
Leonardo
da Vinci

The Wisdom of Leonardo da Vinci

Translated by WADE BASKINS

BARNES & NOBLE
BOOKS
NEW YORK

Originally published as Leonardo da Vinci: Philosophical Diary

Copyright © 1959 by The Philosophical Library

This edition published by Barnes & Noble, Inc.,
by arrangement with The Philosophical Library, Inc.

2004 Barnes & Noble Books

ISBN 0-7607-5286-9

Printed and bound in China

04 05 06 07 08 09 MC 9 8 7 6 5 4 3

REFERENCES

A—M MSS in the library of the Institut de France. Published by Ravaisson-Mollien, Paris, 1881-1891.

An. A Anatomical MSS A in the Windsor Castle Library. Published by T. Sabachnikoff, Paris, 1898.

An. B Anatomical MSS B in the Windsor Castle Library. Published by T. Sabachnikoff, Turin, 1901.

An. C *Quaderni d'Anatomia,* anatomical drawings. Published in six volumes by Vangensten, Fonahn, and Hipstock, Christiania, 1911-1916.

Ar. MS marked Arundel 263 in the British Museum. Published by Danesi, Rome, for the Reale Commissione Vinciana, 1923-1930.

Ash. MSS in the library of Lord Ashburnham, Ashburnham Place, Sussex. Published together with A—M above. Revised edition published by the Reale Commissione Vinciana, Rome, 1938-1941.

Bo. *Trattato della Pittura,* treatise on painting compiled from different MSS and first published by R. Du Fresne, Paris, 1651. Italian text published by A. Borzelli, Lanciano, 1914.

C. A. *Codex Atlanticus,* codex in the Ambrosiana Library in Milan. Published in eight folio volumes by Ulrico Hoepli, Milan, for the Reale Accademia dei Lincei, 1894-1904.

For. MSS in the Forster Library, Victoria and Albert Museum, South Kensington. Published by Danesi, Rome, for the Reale Commissione Vinciana, 1936.

Lei. MS in the library of Lord Leicester at Holkham Hall, Norfolk. Published by G. Calvi, Milan, 1909.

Lu. *Trattato della Pittura,* treatise on painting based in part on the MS *Cod. Vat. Urbinas 1270* (published in facsimile by Princeton University Press in 1956) in the Vatican Library. Published by H. Ludwig, Vienna, 1882.

Triv. MS in the Trivulzi Palace, Milan. Published by L. Beltrami, Milan, 1891; also published by N. De Toni, Milan, 1939.

V. U. *Volo degli Uccelli,* treatise on the flight of birds in the Royal Library, Turin. Published in facsimile by Sabachnikoff, Paris, 1893.

W. Collection of drawings in the Windsor Castle Library. A *Catalogue* prepared by Sir Kenneth Clark was published in two volumes by the Cambridge University Press in 1935-1937.

The most comprehensive collection of Leonardo's work available in English is that prepared by Edward MacCurdy and published by George Braziller, New York, 1955. John Francis Rigaud's translation of the treatise on painting has recently been reissued under the title *The Art of Painting,* Philosophical Library, New York, 1957.

CONTENTS

INTRODUCTION

The intellectual giant who dominated the High Renaissance and stood as a bridge between the medieval and the modern mind moved irresolutely through the burgeoning cities of his native peninsula—Florence, Milan, Mantua, Rome—before he finally found repose in an alien land. Psychologist, zoologist, linguist, botanist, anatomist, geologist, musician, sculptor, architect, critic, civil and military engineer—the complete list would read like a glossary of the professions and areas of specialization of the Fifteenth Century—this many-sided genius who felt that his hand could never elaborate the perfect creations of his mind, without fully realizing it, stood his ground in a dozen different arenas and succeeded in laying the basis for a philosophical system that set him apart from his contemporaries and marked him as the oracle of a new age.

Most of our information about Leonardo da Vinci (1452-1519) comes from his notebooks. His earliest biographer, Giorgio Vasari collected a vast amount of material but failed to examine his findings critically or to present them objectively; though many of the legends set down by Vasari still survive, the compendious notebooks left by Leonardo have made it possible to weed out hearsay and to trace in its broad outlines the remarkable career of this legendary figure. His cryptic, mirror-like script and illustrative sketches cover thousands of pages in codices scattered throughout the western world; until recently, however, his vast legacy was accessible to only a handful of people. Fortunately, in the last half-century facsimile reproductions of his writings on diverse subjects, his accounts of expenditures and commissions, and his notes on his readings and random interests have enabled scholars to paint a fascinating portrait of the master portraitist of all time.

Ser Piero, though a member of a prominent family, reflected no credit on his ancestors in the town of Vinci by

1

becoming involved with a menial girl and bringing into the world a love-child. The taint of illegitimacy was light and did not usually prevent a child born out of wedlock from sharing in the privileges and responsibilities of family life, but there is little evidence to suggest that Leonardo ever enjoyed a normal family life in the home of his father or that he ever had any emotional ties with any of his relatives other than the uncle who showed him kindness and evidenced an interest in his talent; his notebooks reveal no chagrin over his being disinherited by his father, no elation over his being made the sole heir of his uncle, but it is significant that he brutally recorded twice the death of his father, and that each time he advanced him one year in age and set down the wrong day.

"The Challenge to Explore" [1] relates the fascination which a cave held for Leonardo and describes the way in which he was gripped by both fear and longing: "fear of the dark, ominous cavern; longing to see if inside there was something wonderful." Fear of the mystery that life enfolds, the desire to study, paint, and bring to life its wonders—this two-pronged instrument was to result in many discoveries and creations.

Little is known about his conduct and progress in school, but his overpowering passion for searching out the mysterious is evident on every page of his notebooks. It would almost seem that he preferred the mysterious world of nature to the calm routine of a school room and that his relation to nature was closer than his relation to family and friends— that nature even compensated for the maternal love denied him during his tender years. Some of his biographers have assumed that because he became so engrossed with nature and the world of his imagination, he could not find time for regular schooling and that he was to suffer throughout his lifetime on account of his deficiencies.

But Leonardo's frequent complaints about his lack of

---

[1] Titles of sections and selections are interpolated for the convenience of the reader.

education may emphasize not so much his failure to master the three R's as his contempt for the supercilious humanists of his day who held, as Alberti put it, that "a nobleman by birth who is without education—*sanza lectere*—is no more than a peasant." Even though he may not have progressed beyond the elementary phase of his formal education and even though his few years of schooling may have been punctuated by frequent excursions into the surrounding countryside, his knowledge in any of a dozen areas was enough to put to shame many a bigoted humanist.

From earliest childhood Leonardo would sketch his impressions of the things that he saw during his rovings, exulting in his ability to capture graphically and thereby to understand the manifold manifestations of mysterious and enticing Nature. For a child from a middle-class family to study drawings was not unusual, but from the outset this precocious child exhibited remarkable talent; he drew with singular precision and with uncanny realism. A dragon which he once painted was so realistic that his father, startled and at first convinced that it was real, gave serious thought to having him apprenticed to a painter. Ser Piero, who was then serving as legal adviser to artists and their patrons in Florence, knew something of the difficulties that lined the path of an aspiring artist. He therefore first showed some of his son's drawings to Andrea del Verrocchio.

Verrocchio was among the first to suggest and to epitomize something which Leonardo repeatedly proclaimed in his notebooks: the painter is much more than a craftsman; he does not imitate, he creates. During the quattrocento painters and sculptors were rated no higher than artisans and craftsmen; the Ghirlandaio brothers ate the scraps from the table when they worked at the monastery of Passignano; and even a generation after the contributions of Leonardo, Michelangelo, and Raphael, Castiglione noted in *Il Cortegiano* that while the ideal courtier should include painting among his accomplishments, this was not a suitable profession for a man of quality.

Leonardo began his apprenticeship at the age of eighteen. Verrocchio instilled in his most renowned pupil the ingredients that were to influence his whole career—an appreciation of form and a pattern of industry. Painting, under the stimulus of a master craftsman and consummate artist, was to color all his thinking and writing and to forge a fateful link between his name and the history of art. At twenty he joined the painters' guild but stayed on with his teacher; legend has it that when the ambidextrous pupil added one small figure to the master's canvas and surpassed him in skill, Verrocchio laid aside forever his paint-brush; the truth is that their admiration for each other held them together for four years after Leonardo had ended his apprenticeship.

Leonardo apparently after the first flush of success cultivated the friendship of those he most admired, the talented youths of his circle. His serious comments on the depravity of man, his complaints against the evil in their hearts, his predilection for scenes of massive destruction—all relate to a subsequent period in his life. For these youths whose friendship probably satisfied an emotional need rooted deep in his austere childhood, he performed tricks and culled from his readings and conversations the jokes and harmless riddles carefully entered in his notebooks. Soon he was respected and credited with being the most learned member of his circle. And he had every reason to be envied and admired by his acquaintances: he was brilliant, talented, handsome. His later self-portraits suggest but do not capture the physical features of this god-like youth whose "radiant mien," according to Vasari, "brought refreshment to every downcast spirit."

But his heroic features and rare mixture of innate qualities that made him welcomed and envied at first by all the members of his artistic circle were useless to him in his hour of need. In 1476, charged with immorality by an anonymous informer, he was deserted by his friends and relatives. Defenseless, he was pilloried publicly and forced to retreat once more in solitude from the world of men. One can sense the depth of his injury in his diatribes against the monstrous acts of human beings and in the suffering which he wills on them in such imaginary writings as "The Survivors."

Time gradually lessened his suffering; those who had

4

turned away from him in his hour of need began to try to make amends; as a result he was eventually given important commissions and assignments. His shattered faith in humanity somewhat restored, he looked for greater conquests. Here his musical talent, which sometimes evoked more favorable comment than his accomplishments in painting, enabled him to meet the man who was to be his patron for more than a decade.

At the age of thirty he set out for Milan armed with confidence and a lyre in the shape of a horse's head; his confidence was expressed in the form of a letter setting forth as his qualifications feats which would stagger the imagination of anyone who glimpsed their significance, and his lyre was the gift of Lorenzo Il Magnifico to Lodovico Sforza. His proposals, if heard, were doubtlessly not understood by Il Moro (Lodovico); the ruler of Milan could not conceive of pontoon bridges, jet-propelled projectiles, gas shells, armored cars, and battleships. "Methods of Remaining Under Water" contains the statement that Leonardo did not dare to reveal his method of remaining submerged for as long as he could go without food "on account of the base nature of men," but his submarine could hardly be expected to claim more lives than the items mentioned in his appeal to the obdurate duke. He seemed from the beginning to be a second Cassandra either ignored or scoffed at by an unappreciative public. Only centuries later did hindsight reveal that material limitations had blocked the practical application of his ideas in a number of widely divergent fields—sanitation, hydraulics, aeronautics, and engineering, to name but a few.

After many dark and trying months, he managed to win the confidence of Il Moro and to receive several important commissions. Even as he worked on his assignments and produced other works of art independently, his notebooks indicate that he was passionately interested in anatomy, botany, optics, mechanical inventions, and mathematics. And in Florence, despite initial handicaps and later temptations, his conduct was exemplary. In an age that gave first place to smutty stories, obscene language, erotic comments, and intemperance, he remained sober, confident always of his mental and physical powers of resistance. His private life was a paragon of orderliness and industry. He had developed a revulsion to wanton gratification of the senses and sought with philosophical calm to prove by his actions that the key to a long and productive life is the sublimation of physical desires and the cultivation of the mental faculties. It is in this context that his writings on the good life, especially his aphorisms, breathe originality.

To the years of his association with Lodovico is due his acquaintance with people who were to have a permanent influence on him all during his quest for a unified philosophy of life. Among the brilliant young men with whom he was associated were the geometrician Luca Pacioli and the anatomist Marcantonio. Still, at every turn the fame which seemed to hover over him eluded him before the moment of triumph. Though he had been entrusted by Lodovico with important commissions and was consulted on many issues, ranging from architectural works in Padua (where he frequented a good library) to fortification of the ducal palace in Milan, the project which focused attention on him from all sides was never realized. Commissioned to produce an equestrian statue of Lodovico's father, he drew up plans for a colossal figure; homage rained upon him, and his projected monument was called the eighth wonder of the world; but before his statue could be cast, the metal set aside for this purpose was used for cannon.

It was during the same period that he accepted as an apprentice without fee the ephebus Giacomo Caprotti, who clung to him as a shadow throughout most of the remainder of his life. It was also during the same period that he produced (in collaboration with Ambrogio and Evangelista de Predis) his celebrated altarpiece, the "Virgin of the Rocks." Toward the end of his stay in Milan, he painted his famous "Last Supper," the most perfect embodiment of his theories on art.

Shortly after he seemed to have gained some measure of fame and security, however, the French brought about the downfall of his patron and shattered his dreams. After Lodovico was forced to flee before the invading French,

Leonardo went briefly to Mantua, where he resisted the spell of Isabella d'Este, the foremost lady in the world of arts in that day, then on to Venice, where he apparently carried out military engineering assignments.

April, 1500, found him back in Florence, rich but not famous. At forty-eight he was still strong, muscular, and erect; his weathered face and sunken cheeks, however, made him appear much older. His overt actions were in sharp contrast to his meticulous attentiveness to detail in the privacy of his notebooks; he affected the typical Florentine air of liberality and played the part of the *grand seigneur* in his dealings with outsiders, but in his notebooks he carefully itemized his expenditures and credits.

For two years (1502-1503) he worked for Cesare Borgia, executed or undertook the execution of several works of art, and finally as a result of the praise lavished on his "Mona Lisa" on which he had worked for three or four years (1503-1506) and which is of course the most celebrated portrait of all time, was named court painter to Louis XII. Given a leave of absence by the Florentines to complete his "Virgin of the Rocks," he went to Milan and remained there for seven years. During this period he continued his anatomical studies and compiled a treatise on the flight of birds. During this period he also established an enduring friendship with Francesco Melzi, a youth apprenticed to him by an aristocratic family. Francesco had little talent but a heart of gold; drawn intuitively to the aging genius, the worshipful youth was to show him unfailing solicitude during his remaining years.

In September of 1513, shortly after the defeat of the French, he left Milan and started to Rome in the company of Lorenzo de' Medici, Giacomo, and Francesco. A second Medici, Giovanni, had been elected pope, but it was yet another Medici, Giuliano, who gave Leonardo a room in the Vatican and paid him a salary. There Leonardo soon gained a reputation as an eccentric, for he could frequently be seen throwing little inflated animals up into the air and watching them swerve up and down before falling; observers did not suspect that he was discovering some important

7

principles of aerodynamics. Despite his high hopes, he received only minor commissions while in the Vatican, and these mostly from foreigners; moreover, he had difficulty with those who regularly worked with him. He had hoped that the election of Giovanni to the papacy would mark the advent of the golden age for all the artists, but Leo X overlooked the man who had already created more than his share of the world's masterpieces of art in favor of Raphael. In a final attempt to win favor and put an end to the complaints of those who were helping him in his work (the making of mirrors), he put together a treatise on speech—now lost—and sent it to the pope; failing to achieve the recognition which he felt to be his due, he made preparations to leave. In his notebook he wrote: "The Medici made me and ruined me."

In 1515 he returned to Milan, where he became court painter to Francis I. The French king, who sought always to surround himself with the accoutrements of learning, commissioned him to buy back all his paintings and persuaded him to accompany his court to France. Leonardo settled in Castel Cloux, near Amboise. The king was a frequent visitor and took great pleasure in conversing with the Italian sage, even to the point of monopolizing his time and keeping him from his work; for although his right hand was now paralyzed, he continued to write, sketch, and paint with his left hand (which he had always used by preference anyway), and to direct a number of students in their tasks. Cellini recorded that he heard the king say that "he did not believe any other man had ever been born into the world who knew so much as Leonardo, not only in sculpture, painting and architecture, but still more in that he was a great philosopher."

But Leonardo was never fully aware of his own intellectual stature. Distressed by the thought that his life was a maze of fragmentary achievements, he turned during his last years to the comforts of religion. He has been wrongly criticized for putting his philosophy above Christ; it would be more accurate to say as an unbiased observer who revered life in all its manifestations he rebelled against the literal, narrow-minded interpretations of his contemporaries, mocked their hair-splitting arguments, and pointed an accusing finger at the abuses of Christianity—the debasement of priests, the sale of indulgences, chicanery, pomp, and hypocrisy.

The last chapter of his life was recorded by those who visited him at Castle Cloux. A self-imprisoned exile in a foreign land, he counted himself a failure. The man who painted the most perfect portrait, fashioned the most beautiful fresco, and designed an equestrian statue ranked by his contemporaries as the eighth wonder of the world, died neglected by the world that molded and checked his thought. Not a single fragment of his notebooks had been published; as a result, posterity had to learn afresh the facts he had accumulated and the laws that he had adumbrated. The noblest attempt of man to penetrate and absorb every field of knowledge came to an end on May 2, 1519.

Legend has it that a king held his head during his last hours, but the truth is that this honor was reserved not for the high priest of the Renaissance in France but for Francesco Melzi, the altruistic countryman who had sought through his solicitude to mitigate the lot of a man for whom time was always out of joint. Francis I cried at the news of the death of Leonardo, but only Francesco, to whom his idol had entrusted his writings and sketches, could record with partial understanding and whole-hearted sincerity: "The death of Leonardo is a loss to everyone; it is not in the power of nature to reproduce such another man."

Leonardo had the artist's power of observation coupled with the scientist's intuition. Though in some instances he appears to have stood alone and to have anticipated discoveries by centuries, it is as wrong to attribute to him all the inventions and conclusions revealed by the hindsight of modern science as to withhold from him credit for the giant strides which he took independently despite the handicaps imposed on him by his age.

The dreams, accomplishments, and failures recorded in his notebooks can be understood and appreciated only in terms of his age. His was the age in which humanism, far from having penetrated all layers of society, had reached

9

only the elite, whom it tyrannized. Denied direct access to the classics which constituted the staple fare of the humanists and embittered by their contempt for knowledge based on experience, he nevertheless used their discoveries to introduce a new era in the history of painting, a field in which he knew no superior.

Humanism by emphasizing antiquity focused attention on the human form and divorced the fine arts from religion; by freeing painting from religion and turning the attention of the painter outside the church, it brought about the discovery of the very reality which its exponents had disclaimed and which Leonardo embraced. He was quick to grasp the byproduct of their speculation and to champion it as the master of their authors and the source of their authority.

He militated against those who labeled him an uneducated man. He ridiculed the fantastic arguments practiced by the members of the Platonic Academy on the nature of the soul and condemned those who trumpeted the works of others, yet ignored his findings, which were based on experience rather than on authority. He tried always to prove (as in his "Foreword" and throughout "Student and Philosopher") that his tested knowledge was superior to their speculation and to make them aware of the emptiness of their book learning; because of the control which the humanists exercised throughout society, however, he felt at times that his struggle was hopeless. Even the most erudite of his contemporaries failed to realize that the man whom they labeled *sanza lectere* surpassed them all in the range and depth of his knowledge. For though he had the dreams of a god, the peculiar orientation and limited resources of his age chained him to the ground in all practical matters and allowed and encouraged him to soar unfettered only in the sphere thought least worthy of a man of quality, painting.

Though he made the most of the human side of humanism, on the metaphysical side he fell into some deep pitfalls and never actually succeeded in freeing himself completely from the folderol of the Schoolmen. For instance, much of his writing is vitiated by his failure to draw a clearcut distinction between mental and physical phenomena; in addi-

10

tion, the metaphysical concept of the microcosm and the macrocosm—the parallelism between the body of man and the body of the universe—pervaded much of his thinking; indeed, it was years before he succeeded in casting aside the weight of tradition and espousing without reserve the lucidity of mathematical reasoning.

Some of the statements found in his notebooks sound colorless and pedestrian today even though they were remarkably ingenious at the time. Water, for instance, was generally assumed to rise under pressure of the wind above the height of mountains since it is lighter than earth; Pliny the elder taught that it circulates through the veins of the earth; Aristotle held that it is locked in the bowels of the earth; against this, Leonardo relied on experience and reached an independent conclusion. The scholastics gave to every explanation a theological interpretation; Leonardo studied the facts and sought the underlying cause. The pneuma according to Galen are designed to supply the organs of the body with energy; Leonardo, unwilling to accept such reasoning at face value, studied the nerves, arteries, and heart and almost evolved an understanding of the circulation of the blood; nevertheless, the weight of tradition caused him to conceive of body heat as a result of friction of the blood. His age followed Plato in holding that the eye sends out rays which bring back images of concrete things; here he broke completely with tradition and by observation proved the contrary, a theory which was not generally accepted until after his death.

But for the weight of tradition he might have been credited with many other remarkable discoveries adumbrated in his notebooks—the heliocentric theory of the universe, the laws of gravitation, inertia, motion, optics, and so on through sensory perception, the density and elasticity of the air, and capillary action, to cite only the most obvious. There are even statements relating to time which recall the theory of Einstein.

The most remarkable discovery made by Leonardo in the field of science relates, however, not to specific disciplines but to methodology. In his quest for a consistent philosophy

11

of life he had to develop a new method, and this method tore at the very roots of scholastic thought. He had the ability to devise simple experiments that would cut to the heart of a problem (as in the experiment suggested in "The Laws of Motion"), acute powers of observation, and an abiding appreciation for mathematical order; with his constant emphasis on experiment, observation, and mathematics, he had a firmer grasp of the basic principles of scientific method than did the admirers of Sir Francis Bacon a century later. But so great was the weight of tradition that even some of his most remarkable discoveries are marred by hesitation, vacillation, and retrogression; for example, his brilliant observations on the moon led him to the conclusion that the earth is not the center of the universe, but tradition weighed so heavily that he turned back to the geocentric pattern of thinking.

Even as his awareness of the conflict between his independent way of thinking and the mental science of the Schoolmen increased and even as he expressed his confidence in the superiority of his own method, his most ambitious plans were likely to be thwarted by material factors. Typical is his dream of flight, which became almost an obsession with him; a boyhood dream had inspired him with the will to devise some means of flying; hoping to confer immortality on himself and on his native town, he made countless designs and conducted numerous preliminary experiments in aeronautics; several years before his death, however, his dream shattered, he stopped recording plans and designs in his notebooks. The man who was accomplished in more fields than any other man of his age was forced to admit failure, not because of any fallacy in his thinking but because he lacked the material means—in this instance a motor—to perfect his ideas.

His understanding of the method of science is amply illustrated in his anatomical studies. His drawings of the internal structure of the human body are accurate and are instructive even today. For centuries they were unsurpassed. In "Comparative Anatomy" he records that for his drawing he dissected not one but a number of corpses, all according to a preconceived plan.

Both his grasp of the basic principles of the scientific method and his application of these principles in his anatomical studies command respect, but he is best remembered as the titan of the world of painting. Each of the eight extant works indisputably attributed to him bears the stamp of genius.

He aimed to paint man and the intention of his soul. He mastered the atmosphere of the physical surroundings; he managed also to catch the mystical, sympathetic side of the human face—in short, to lay bare the secret soul. His dual aim resulted in a two-fold contribution to the art of painting: an illusion of a third dimension through mastery of the technique of light and shade, and the use of gestures and facial expressions to convey the intention of the soul to the mind of the viewer. To perfect his art, he methodically studied deaf mutes and learned how to characterize figures as much by their actions as by their features. The fruit of his studies is revealed in all of his paintings but especially in the "Last Supper," where his heroic figures enact twelve different dramas based upon a single emotion. His paintings influenced a whole generation of painters; his pioneering techniques soon became commonplace devices.

This disorganized genius unfortunately robbed the world of countless masterpieces by stopping frequently on the threshold of a solution. In him the creative urge found fulfillment in the concept rather than in its realization. Not infrequently he would start a project, make several rough outlines, reach a solution, then before applying the finishing touches, turn his attention to a new project. Many seminal ideas, in art and in other fields, were lost or abandoned, not so much because he lacked the mental discipline or patience to finish a project, but because new interests constantly supplanted the old ones. In his notebooks the erratic pattern of his thought is revealed on every page; he repeatedly outlined plans and set down ideas for many books but never managed to publish a single volume during his lifetime; moreover, it is hard to find in his whole collection of notes, observations, plans, and literary works a single passage in which two paragraphs seem logically to follow each other. In his attempt to instruct painters in "The Flood," for example, he soon gives vent to his anguish and inveighs against the injustices he suffered at the hands of an unsympathetic public.

The first of his writings to attract attention was composed for his own pupils as well as for later painters and contained rules of conduct as well as instructions for painting. As noted earlier, some of his non-technical writings were outright plagiarisms while others—especially those that express in disguised form sentiments which could not have been aired openly—are of his own devising. Guessing games in which everyday events were dressed up in abstruse language and passed off as prophecies, story-telling, and polite conversation were part and parcel of everyday life during the quattrocento. Leonardo must have searched through more than one Bestiarius and Physiologus to compile his strange assortment of stories—stories completely out of character with the body of his writings and inserted like the ruins of a crumbling society into the emerging structure of his new philosophy. Whether invented or plagiarized, his fables had but one eternal theme, the punishment of pride, ambition, and envy; in the same vein, he used his horror stories to give expression to emotions that he may have felt but would never have dared to voice in real-life situations.

He apologized repeatedly for his lack of formal education, yet he captures the reader's attention by his vivid imagination, his straightforward style, and his command of the Italian lexicon. And though he struggled unsuccessfully with grammar, his pointed style, his ability always to select from the gamut of his vocabulary the *mot juste*, and the intensity of his feeling all endear him to the modern reader. Like others of his century, he imbued even his narrative passages with an aphoristic tinge. More important still, because of the strength, clarity, and charm of his style, he deserves a place of honor among the first writers of true Italian prose.

Even apart from his discoveries in anatomy, astronomy, painting, and all the other arts and sciences referred to in his notebooks, this Italian brother of Faust, as he has been

14

called, would still deserve a niche in the pantheon of the divinely inspired, for he stands as a symbol of man's unending pursuit of an elusive goal, the understanding and appreciation of his universe.

But far too long I have already withheld reader from writer, thinker from philosopher. The selections included in this small volume will have served their purpose if they whet the reader's curiosity and introduce him to the man who today would feel at home in any land.

WADE BASKIN

Southern State College

FOREWORD

This journal, begun in Florence in the home of Piero di Baccio Martelli on March 22, 1508, will be a collection of random quotations from many papers which I have written in the hope of ordering them later according to the subjects dealt with. I fear that before I complete my task I shall have to burden the reader by repeating the same things many times, for things are many and memory can not keep them all in store and say: "This I shall not write, for I have already written it." To avoid the mistake of repeating something said before, I should have in each instance to reread everything already written, especially when intervening intervals are long. (Ar. 1 r.)

❖

Realizing that I am unable to seize upon any matter of great usefulness or delight because men born before me have already claimed all useful and necessary themes, I shall do as he who on account of his poverty comes last to the fair and, unable to provide himself with anything else, takes all those things which were examined and rejected as almost worthless by others. The merchandise that has been disdained and rejected by many buyers I shall place on my weak shoulders, and with it I shall go not through huge cities but through poor villages, handing it out and charging whatever it is worth! (C. A. 119 v.)

❖

There are so many words in my mother tongue that I complain about my failure to comprehend things well rather than about the available words from which I might choose to express my ideas clearly. (An. C, II, 16 r.)

❖

I know that many men will say that this is a useless work. They are the ones about whom Demetrius said that he paid no more attention to the wind driven from their mouths by words than to that driven from their lower parts. They are the men who desire only material wealth and luxury, and who do not thirst after knowledge, the food and truly worthy treasure of the soul. For just as the soul is more worthy than the body, so are the riches of the soul more worthy than those of the body. And often when I see one of these men with one of my works in his hand, I am not sure whether he will put it to his nose like a monkey or ask me if it is good to eat. (C. A. 119 v.)

✧

I also know well that since I am no scholar, to many a presumptuous man it will seem reasonable to condemn me as uncouth. Stupid people! They do not realize that as Marius answered the Roman patrician I too might reply: "Those who deck themselves out in the achievements of others will not credit me with my own." They will say that since I am not a man of letters I can not express myself clearly on a subject. What they do not know is that my statements are drawn not from words but rather from experience, which was the mistress of those who have written well and therefore the mistress that I elect and cite in every instance. (C. A. 119 v.)

PART ONE

STUDENT AND PHILOSOPHER

The Challenge to Explore

Good men naturally thirst after knowledge. (C. A. 119 v.)

❖

The stormy sea does not make such a great roar when the north wind lashes its foaming waves back and forth between Scylla and Charybdis; nor Stromboli nor Aetna when the pent-up force of burning brimstone rends asunder the great mountain, hurling through the air earth and rocks along with spurting, spewing flame; nor when the red-hot caverns of Aetna release their restive element, belching it forth and scattering it furiously throughout their domain, shooting by preference any obstacle that stands in the path of their unbridled rage.

Urged on by my eagerness to see the many varied and strange forms shaped by artful nature, I wandered for some time among the shady rocks and finally came to the entrance of a great cavern. At first I stood before it dumbfounded, knowing nothing of such a thing; then I bent over with my left hand braced against my knee and my right shading my squinting, deep-searching eyes; again and again I bent over, peering here and there to discern something inside; but the all-embracing darkness revealed nothing.

Standing there, I was suddenly struck by two things, fear and longing: fear of the dark, ominous cavern; longing to see if inside there was something wonderful. (Ar. 155 r.)

❖

True and False Sciences

Many men will rationally allege that my findings conflict with the raw judgment of certain men held in great reverence, and they will not be swayed by the fact that my findings were born of pure and simple experience, the supreme teacher.

My rules will provide a basis for distinguishing the true and the false. You will therefore promise each other only the things which are possible and most moderate, and you will not be veiled by ignorance but will so act that, even if you miss your mark, you will not give yourself over in desperation to melancholy. (C. A. 119 v.)

Originators and Imitators

Though I can not like others cite authors, I shall cite something much greater and more worthy: experience, the mistress of their masters. They go about capacious and pompous, decked out not in their own performances but in the accomplishments of others; and they will not credit me with my own. If they disdain me as an inventor, how much more blame might be cast on the trumpeters and expositors of the works of others.

There is but one way to judge and appraise men who are true inventors and interpreters to nature and men in contrast to those who are the trumpeters and expositors of the works of others. They are like objects placed in front of a mirror with respect to their likenesses in the mirror; one group is in itself something and the other nothing. People without close ties to nature and garbed only in the inventions of others I should class with animals. (C. A. 117 r.)

Talent and Letters

Whoever cites authority in a discussion is using not his wit but his memory.

Good writing comes from good talent. Since more praise is given to causes than to effects, you should praise good talent without letters more than a man of letters without talent. (C. A. 76 r.)

Authority and Experience

Consider, readers, what we should accept from our forebears. They tried to define soul and life, things that are not demonstrable, but for many centuries they ignored or misunderstood things that were always demonstrable through experience. The eye, which clearly has experience as its function, has up until my time been defined by many authors in but one way; I find through experience that it must be given another definition. (C. A. 119 v.)

Effect of My Rules

If you should ask me: "What issues from your rules? Of what use are they?" I should answer that they restrain inventors and investigators, preventing them from promising to themselves or to others impossible things and thus being called fools or frauds. (C. A. 337 r.)

Necromancy and Alchemy

But of all methods of reasoning, the one to be reckoned most foolish is that relating to necromancy, the sister of alchemy, which works with simple natural elements. Necromancy is even more reprehensible than alchemy inasmuch as it spawns only its own likeness, lies, for these have no part in alchemy. The task of the alchemists can not be carried out by nature since she lacks the organic tools to produce independently the things which man fashions with his hands, such as glass.

Necromancy, however, is a standard or banner unfurled to the wind; it directs the foolish crowd which forever bears witness with its incessant barking to the enduring appeal of such arts. Books are filled with accounts of potent spells and of spirits that speak without tongues or vocal organs, both of which are necessary for speech. They speak, carry heavy weights, make storms and rain; men turn into cats, wolves, and other beasts; the first to turn into fools, however, are those who make such statements.

Surely if necromancy were possible, as vulgar minds think, nothing else in the whole world would be of such great importance for the use and abuse of man. Suppose that in such arts there were the power to trouble the calm serenity of the air, to give the air the darkness of night, to produce storms and winds with frightful thunderclaps and flashes of lightning that rend the darkness and with relentless winds topple tall buildings and uproot forests, causing them to fall upon armies and dash them to the ground, and to produce still other ruinous storms that deprive the farmer of the fruits of his labor. O what manner of war could inflict so much harm on the enemy and even have the power to deprive him of his harvest? What maritime battle could rival the one in which the necromancer commanded the winds and caused every fleet to be sunk and destroyed?

Surely whoever commanded such spurious powers would be master of the people, and no human mind could resist his destructive might. The hidden treasures and gems that lie in the bosom of the earth would all be manifest to him; no lock, no impregnable fortress, but only the necromancer's fancy would spare his foes. He would have himself borne through the air from east to west and in every opposing direction throughout the universe. But why go further? What would such an artisan be unable to overcome? Almost nothing except death.

I am merely suggesting the harm and the good that might be contained in such an art if it were true. And if it were true, why would it not be practiced by the men who worship it, regardless of any divinity? I know that countless men to satisfy their appetites would destroy God and the whole universe. If it is not still practiced by the men to whom it is so necessary, then it never was and never will be. The spirit is said to be invisible and incorporeal, but within the elements there is nothing incorporeal; for where there is no body there is void; within the elements void does not exist, for immediately it would be filled by its element. (An. B, 31 v.)

Spirits

A spirit is by definition a power joined to a body. Alone it can not support itself, nor can it make any sort of movement. And if you say that it supports itself, this can not be from within the elements, for if the spirit is an incorporeal quantity, then this quantity is designated as void, and does not exist in nature; even if it did, it would be filled through the destruction of the element in which it was created. (An. B 312)

✧

There can be no voice where there is not movement and trembling of the air; there can be no trembling of the air where there is no instrument; and there can be no incorporeal instrument. Since that is so, a spirit can have neither voice nor form nor force, and should it take possession of a body, it would be unable to penetrate or enter through closed doors. It is claimed that by means of accumulated and compressed air spirits gain possession of variously shaped bodies and through these instruments acquire strength for speech and motion. I hold that where there are no nerves and bone, no force can be exercised by any movement made by the imagined spirit.

Shun the teachings of those speculators whose arguments are not confirmed by experience. (B, 4 v.)

Speech and Languages

No other member has need of so many muscles as the tongue. Twenty-four have been noted, and I have found still others. Of all the members that are moved voluntarily, this one has the greatest number of movements.

And if you wish to give first place to the eye, which receives all the images from the numberless figures and colors of the objects placed before it, or to the nose, which identifies numberless blends of odors, or to the ear, which perceives various sounds, I shall say that the tongue also senses numberless simple and compound savors. But that is irrelevant since I have proposed to treat only of the locomotion of each member.

Only consider how by means of the movement of the tongue, with the aid of the lips and teeth, the pronunciation of all the names of things is made known and the simple and compound words of languages reach our ears; and these

23

words—since every manifestation as well as every one of the numberless actual and potential phenomena of nature has a name—would stretch to infinity; and names are expressed not in one language but in countless languages since they vary continuously from century to century and from country to country through the intermingling of peoples who by war or chance are continuously brought together; and these very languages are doomed to oblivion and are mortal like other created things; and if our world is eternal, these languages have varied and will continue to vary in numberless ways on account of the numberless centuries that are contained in infinite time. (An. B 28 v.)

Creativity in Nature and in Man

The situation is different in the case of all the other senses. They are concerned only with things continuously produced by nature, and nature does not vary the common species of the things which she creates. From time to time the things created by man, the greatest instrument of nature, do vary. Nature stops with the production of simple elements; with these elements man produces numberless compounds. But man lacks the power to create any simple element except another self: his children. Proof of this is that the ancient alchemists never either by chance or by deliberate experiment succeeded in creating the least thing that can be created by nature.

Unstinted praise is due those who invent things for the use of men. These inventors would merit still more praise if they were not inventors of noxious things, like poison and other similar destroyers of life or mind. But they are not guiltless. With patient study and industry they try to create not the least noble product of nature but the most excellent, namely gold, the true child of the sun; more than any other thing it is like the sun, and nothing created is more eternal than this gold. . . .

If foolish greed causes you to make such a mistake, why not go to the mines where nature produces gold and there become her disciple? This will surely cure you of your stupidity, for you will see that nothing which you have wrought in fire is used by nature in creating gold. There is no quicksilver, no sulphur of any kind, no fire, no heat other than that of nature, the generatrix of our world. . . .

And note that here is a vegetative soul, something you are powerless to create. (An. B 28 v.)

Perpetual Motion

O you who speculate on perpetual motion, how many vain designs have resulted from your quests! Join the ranks of those who search for the philosopher's stone! (For. II, 92 v.)

✧

No insentient thing will move by itself, and when it does move it must be set in motion by unequal forces, that is, by inequality in time, in movement, or in weight; and when the movement of the first motor is checked, immediately the second will cease. (A 22 v.)

Truth, Perception, and Nature

Truth was always but the daughter of time. (M. 58 v.)

✧

O you who speculate on things, take no pride in knowing the things that nature by herself designs but joy in knowing the designs of those things that are devised by your minds. (G. 47 r.)

✧

The lying interpreters of nature affirm that quicksilver is the semen common to all metals, but they forget that nature varies her semen according to the diversity of the things that she wishes to bring forth into the world. (C. A. 76 v. a)

✧

All knowledge begins with perception. (Triv. 20 v.)

✧

The senses are material; the intellect transcends them when it contemplates. (Triv. 33 v.)

Mental things that have not been derived through the senses are vain, and nothing but harmful truth is born of them. Because their reasonings are born of intellectual poverty, such speakers are always poor; and if born rich they die poor in their old age, for it seems that nature takes vengeance on those who seek to work miracles. They have less than other more modest men, while those that seek to become rich in one day live for a long time in great poverty. This happens and will happen throughout eternity to the alchemists, who seek to create gold and silver; to those who endeavor to make dead water come alive and create perpetual motion; and to the most stupid, necromancers and magicians. (An. 1, 13 v.)

Knowledge and Reason

It is said that knowledge is mechanical when engendered by experience, scientific when it has its beginning and its end in the mind, and semi-mechanical when born of science and brought to an end mechanically. But to me all knowledge is vain and fraught with errors unless it is born of experience, the mother of all certainty, or unless it results in a definite experience—in other words, unless in the beginning, in the intermediate stage, or at the end it passes through one of the five senses. And if we entertain doubts about the certainty of each thing that passes through the senses, how much more ought we to doubt things hostile to the senses, such as the essence of God and of the soul and similar things about which people are always arguing and fighting. In fact, it happens that wrangling always arises where reason is wanting but not where there is certainty.

Where there is wrangling there is no true science, for there is but one word for truth; once made known, however, truth forever silences all wrangling; and wherever wrangling springs up again, there is found not the certainty of science but falsehood and confusion.

In every true science experience has penetrated through the senses and imposed silence on the tongues of the disputants. Its disciples pasture not on dreams but always on basic and known principles. They move forward step by step, making valid deductions all the way, as is evidenced in the elementary mathematical sciences: numbers and measures, called arithmetic and geometry . . . . Here it is not argued that two threes make more or less than six, nor that a triangle has fewer than two right angles; here every argument is lost in eternal silence and scholarship is crowned with peace. This is never true of false mental sciences. (Lu. 33)

Nature and Experience

Leonardo da Vinci is the disciple of experience. (C. A. 259 r.)

✧

He who promises of experience more than is in it goes counter to reason. (C. A. 299 r. b)

✧

And so, speculators, mistrust authors who have tried to make themselves interpreters between nature and men by using nothing more than imagination. Trust only those who have exercised their minds not on the proofs of nature but on the results of their own experiments.

Experiences deceive those who are not familiar with their natures; often those that seem the same differ greatly. (I. 102 r.)

✧

Before I go any further I shall perform an experiment, for my intention is first to cite an experiment and then by reason to demonstrate why it is constrained to work as it does.

This is the rule by which those who speculate on natural effects must proceed. Though nature begins with reason and ends with experiment, we must follow the opposite course: we must (as I said earlier) begin with an experiment and with that investigate the reason. (E. 55 r.)

✧

Experience never errs; only our judgment errs, promising of experience things which are not in its power.

Men wrongly complain about experience, violently condemning it and accusing it of being fallacious, but they ought to let experience stand and credit their outcries to their own ignorance which causes them to be led on by their vain and foolish desires and to promise of experience things not in its power. Still they state that it is fallacious.

Men wrongly complain about guiltless experience, accusing it of fallacious and foolish demonstrations. (C. A. 154 r.)

✧

Wisdom is the daughter of experience. (For. III, 14)

✧

Experience, the interpreter between inventive nature and the human race, teaches us that whatever nature is constrained by necessity to create among mortals she can produce only as reason, her rudder, dictates. (C. A. 86 r.)

✧

No action produced by nature can be produced with the same instruments in any shorter manner. (Ar. 175 v.)

✧

One should not be censured for grafting into the scheme of scientific procedure any general rule derived from a previous conclusion. (Ar. 32 v.)

✧

Before you make of a case a general rule, test it two or three times and observe whether all experiments produce identical results. (A. 47 r.)

Mathematics

He who finds fault with the supreme certainty of mathematics pastures on confusion; never can he silence the contradictions of the sophistic sciences which yield nothing but perpetual wrangling. (An. II, 14 r.)

✧

O students, study mathematics and build on a solid foundation. (An. C I, 7 r.)

✧

Unless you are a mathematician, do not read my principles. (An. IV, 14 v.)

✧

No human investigation can claim to be a true science if it is not proven through mathematical demonstrations. If you say that the sciences which have their beginning and their end in the mind contain any truth, this is not supported but denied by many reasons. In the first place, in such reasoning experience does not intervene, and without this there is no certainty. (Lu. 1)

✧

There is no certainty where one of the mathematical sciences can not be applied or where there is no bond with mathematics. (G. 96 v.)

Natural Law and Adaptation

Nature does not break her law. (C. 23. v.)

✧

Nature is bound by her own law; this law animates her. (C. 23. v.)

✧

There is no effect in nature without a cause; grasp the cause and you have no need for experiment. (C. A. 147 v.)

✧

Necessity is the mistress and guardian of nature.

Necessity is the theme and inventor of nature, the brake and eternal rule. (For. III, 43 v.)

✧

Every body is composed of those members and humors necessary for its subsistence. This necessity is well known and is provided for by the soul which has elected such a corporeal form for its temporary habitation.

Observe the fish which through the continuous contact that it of necessity makes with the water is fitted by its soul, the daughter of nature, to exude through the pores

29

found between its overlapping scales a certain viscous sweat which is removed with difficulty from the fish and which serves the fish in the same way that pitch serves a ship. (For. III, 38 r.)

✧

The knife, an accidental weapon, has deprived man of the use of his nails, a natural weapon. (An. I, 4 v.)

✧

If nature had laid down a single rule for the character of numbers, the faces of all men would have been so similar that it would be impossible to know one from the other. But she varied the five members of the face; though she followed an almost universal rule with respect to their size, she did not observe the same rule with respect to quality and thereby made it possible to distinguish clearly one face from another. (C. A. 11 v. a)

The Practice of Abridging Works

Write a treatise on the criticism due scholars who interfere with and contract the study of anatomy. (An. I, 4 v.)

✧

Those who abridge works do injury to knowledge and to love, for love of anything is the creature of knowledge, and love is all the more ardent as knowledge is more certain. Certainty is born of integral knowledge of all those parts united to form the whole of the thing to be loved.

Of what worth is it to abbreviate the part of the thing of which a man professes to give an integral account if he leaves out the greater part of the parts that make up the whole?

Impatience, the mother of stupidity, lauds brevity. Impatient people lack the time for gaining complete knowledge of a particular thing, such as a human body, yet they try to embrace the mind of God, which contains the universe, weighing it and cutting it into countless parts as if they wished to study its anatomy!

O stupid creatures! Do you not see that even though

you have been living with yourself all your life, you are still ignorant of the thing that you possess in the highest degree, your madness! And still you wish, with the hosts of sophists, to deceive yourself and others, despising the mathematical sciences which represent true knowledge of all things within their scope and turning your attention to miracles; you write and explain things which are beyond the reach of the human mind and which can not be demonstrated by any natural example; and it seems to you that you have worked a miracle when you have destroyed the work of some inquiring intellect; and you fail to observe that you fall into the same mistake as he who robs the tree of the ornament of its leafy branches laden with odiferous flowers and fruit and shows that many bare boards can be made from the tree!

Justinus, who edited the histories written by Troius Pompeius—who compiled the outstanding accomplishments of his forebears and filled his book with wonderful ornament—composed a bare thing worthy only of impatient minds to whom devoting time to something useful such as the study of works of nature and the works of human beings seems a waste.

But let such people stand in the company of beasts and let their courtesans and associates be dogs and other rapacious animals; always chasing their prey, they go behind the innocent animals that are forced by hunger to come during snowstorms to your homes seeking alms like their protector.[1] (An. II, 14 r.)

Men and Beast

If you are, as you have written, the king of the animals—you ought to say king of the beasts since you are the biggest one of them—why not help them in order that they may later give you their children for the benefit of your gullet, with which you have tried to make of yourself a grave for all

_____

[1] The shift in perspective is characteristic of all of Leonardo's writing.

animals?

Still other truths I should speak if I were permitted to tell the whole truth.

But before we put aside the subject of human things, let me mention a serious evil which does not occur among the animals that eat their own species unless they are mentally deficient—among them as among men lunatics, though not so numerous, do exist—and this happens only among predatory animals such as lions, leopards, panthers, lynxes, and cats, which sometimes eat their young. But you, besides your young, eat your father, mother, brothers and friends, and even this does not suffice, for you go through other islands hunting for and seizing other men; and these after you have emasculated them and fattened them, you send down your gullet. Does not nature produce enough simple foods for you to sate your appetite? And if you are not satisfied with the simple ones, can you not by mixing these make numberless compounds such as those described by Platina and others who have written about food?

And if one is found to be virtuous and good, do not drive him away from you but honor him in order that he will not have to flee from you and retreat into the wilderness or a cave or any other solitary place to escape from your snares. If one is found, honor him as a terrestrial god. Such gods merit from us monument, sculptures, and honors. But I remind you that these images are not to be eaten by you as they are in certain regions of India. When an image is thought to have worked some miracle, a priest cuts it into pieces—they are made of wood—and distributes these pieces throughout the region, and not without recompense.

Each man pulverizes his share and puts it in the first food that he eats; afterwards he is convinced that he has eaten his saint and that the saint will thereafter ward off all dangers. What do you think, man, about your own species? Are you really as wise as you pretend? Are these things that a man ought to do?

Here I know that I will make a few enemies. No one will believe that I am speaking about him, for few are those who find their vices displeasing and the only ones to take offense are those who by nature are opposed to such vices. Many men hate their fathers and become angry with their friends when they reproach them for their vices; examples that are contrary to their practices are worthless to them, as is any human counsel. (An. II, 14 r.)

Theory and Practice

Practice must always be built on good theory. (G. 8 r.)

❖

Science is the captain, practice the soldiers. (I. 130 r.)

❖

Study science first, then persevere in the practice born of this science. (Lu. 54)

❖

Those who become enamored of practices without science are like sailors who go aboard ship without a rudder and compass, for they are never certain where they will land. (G. 8 r)

❖

When you wish to produce an effect with an instrument, do not waste time on many jumbled parts but search the shortest means; do not do as those who, not knowing how to say a thing in their own words, resort to circumlocutions and confused verbiage. (C. A. 206 v.)

❖

Every instrument must be shaped by experience. (G. 8r.)

The Elements of Physics

Force is a spiritual, incorporeal, and invisible potency that is awakened to short life in those bodies which as a result of accidental violence are out of their natural position and state of rest: spiritual I said because in this force is active life; incorporeal and invisible I said because the body that creates it increases in neither weight nor form; short-lived I said because it always tends to overcome its cause, and having done this, dies. (B. 63 r.)

❖

Force has its origin in spiritual motion. This motion, flowing through the members of sentient animals. distends their muscles. Distended, these muscles contract, drawing back with them the nerves attached to them and thus generating force throughout the members of the human body. (Ar. 151 r.)

✧

Gravity, force, and accidental motion together with thrust are the four accidental potencies that account for the life and death of all visible works of mortals. (For. II, 116 v.)

✧

Gravity, force, material motion and thrust are the four accidental potencies which in their wonderful and varied operations in this world seem to the human species like a second nature, for through such potencies all visible works of mortals have their being and their death. (Ar. 151 v.)

✧

Material motion is born of spiritual motion. (Ar. 151 r.)

✧

The more it is exercised, the weaker violent motion becomes. Natural motion behaves in the opposite manner. (Triv. 26 r.)

✧

The starting point of motion is indivisible time, for it originates at the end point of the line of motion created by weight, the cause of thrust. (For. III, 32)

✧

Proportion is found not only in numbers and measures but also in tones, weights, times and places, and in every existing potency. (K. 49 r.)

✧

Mechanics is the paradise of the mathematical sciences; through it one reaches the mathematical fruit. (E. 8 r.)

✧

O wonderful is your justice, First Mover! You have willed that no power lack the processes and qualities necessary for its effects. (A. 24 r.)

34

Laws of Motion

Any spherical body with a thick and resistant surface will move when acted upon by a like force as great a distance on a rebound caused by a hard, solid object as when thrown freely through the air. (A. 24 r.)

✧

Every weight tends to fall toward the center of gravity by the shortest route. (C. 28 v.)

✧

Every heavy body that falls freely moves toward the center of gravity; the heavier part will be closer to the center of the world. (For. II, 51 r.)

✧

The tendency of every heavy body is to make its center the center of the earth. (For. III, 66 v.)

✧

The natural motion of heavy bodies increases in speed by one degree for every degree of fall. Thus its increase in force takes a pyramidal form: every degree of increase in the breadth of the pyramid is matched by a corresponding increase in its length; the proportion of increase corresponds to an arithmetic proportion, for the increases are always equal. (M. 57 v.)

✧

Every heavy body that falls freely moves toward the center of the world. The heaviest body falls fastest, and the longer it falls, the faster it moves. (C. A. 381 v.)

✧

If many bodies of equal weight and form are dropped in regular succession, the increases in their intervals will all be equal. . . .

The experiment to test this hypothesis concerning motion must be conducted in this manner: take two balls of equal weight and size and have them dropped from a great height in such a way that one touches the other at the beginning of their fall; the experimenter, standing on the ground, can see whether or not their fall has kept them together. The experiment should be repeated several times in order to avoid having some accident impede or falsify the findings and thus deceive the investigator. (M. 57 v.)

Bodies in Water and in the Air

The water displaced by a ship is exactly as heavy as the weight of the ship itself. (For. II, 65 v.)

❖

A body exerts as much force against the air as the air against the body. You see how its wings beating against the air sustain a heavy eagle in the thinnest air near the element of fire. You also see the air moving across the water as it presses against the bulging sails and makes the heavily laden ships move swiftly along. From these obvious and demonstrable facts you can learn that man with huge wings joined together can exert sufficient pressure against the resisting air to overcome it, enslave it, and rise above it. (C. A. 381 v.)

How the Wheel Moves

No matter what weight is applied to the wheel to cause it to move, its center will surely act on the center of the wheel's axis. No instrument that human intellect might devise to have the wheel turn with its axis can change this effect.

O you who speculate about perpetual motion, how many vain designs have you created in your search! Class yourselves with those who seek the philosopher's stone. (For. II, 92 v.)

Vibration

I hold that every body that is moved or struck retains for some time the nature of this movement or thrust, and that retention varies according to the greater or lesser force of the blow or motion.

Observe, for example, how a bell when struck retains the noise of the blow or how a stone when ejected by a bombard preserves the nature of its thrust. The sound from a blow against a thick body will last longer than one from a pervious body; and the one that lasts longest will be the one made by a thin suspended body. The eye retains for a while the images of luminous bodies. (Triv. 43 r.)

✧

The ringing of a bell leaves behind the impression of its likeness just as the sun leaves behind the impression of its likeness in the eye or an odor in the air. But it remains to be seen whether the likeness of the blow remains in the bell or in the air, and this you will learn by putting your ear to the surface of the bell after it has been struck.

The blow struck on the bell will resound and will be communicated to another similar bell. In the same way, the vibrating string of a lute will resound and its vibration will be communicated to another similar string that will produce the same note on another lute; this you will see if you place a straw upon the string like the one sounded. (A. 22 v.)

✧

Every blow that remains or seems to remain in the bell after it has been rung is not in the bell but in the hearer's ear, which preserves in itself the likeness of the ringing of the bell and gradually loses it in the same way that the eye loses the impression of the sun as it gradually dissolves and disappears.

If the foregoing propositions were not true, you could not suddenly stop the ringing of a bell by touching it with the palm of your hand, especially at the height of its power. It would be useless to touch the bell after it had been struck, for the ear would still preserve its ringing; but you see that when your hand is placed on the bell, the sound immediately stops. (C. A. 332 v.)

✧

As a stone cast into the water becomes the center and cause of various circles, so a sound made in the air is diffused in circles; so every body placed in luminous air spreads in circles and fills the surrounding air with numberless likenesses of itself, appearing everywhere and in every detail. (A. 8 v.)

❖

An object that is not suspended does not resound; an object that is suspended does resound. A bell vibrates when struck; its rapid vibration makes the surrounding air vibrate and immediately resound; when checked by any slight contact it does not vibrate and the air does not resound. (Triv. 36 r.)

The Nature of Motion

Motion is the cause of all life. (H. 141 r.)

❖

Motion is caused by force and applied to bodies that are removed from their places. (A. 27 v.)

❖

Natural motion was first accidental; that is, the falling stone was first carried or thrown upward. Upward motion is designated as accidental, downward as natural. (A. 4)

The Soul

The motion of earth rebounding against earth moves but little the affected parts. Water struck by water makes circles around the point of contact; over a long distance, sound in the air; further still in fire; and further still in the soul of the universe. But since the mind is finite it does not reach into the infinite. (H 67 r.)

Light Waves and Sound Waves

Every body placed in luminous air radiates its likenesses throughout the numberless parts of the air; it is wholly and everywhere in all its parts; its images become smaller and smaller at equal distances in the surrounding area. . . .

The stone cast into the water becomes the center of various circles that have as their center the point that was disturbed. In the same way, the air is filled with circles whose centers are the noises and sounds made in the air . . .

The stone where it penetrates the surface of the water causes circles to be formed around it, and these circles keep spreading out until they disappear; similarly the air, struck by sounds or noises, spreads out in circles that gradually fade away, so that whoever is nearest understands most and whoever most distant, least. (C. A. 373 r.)

What Is an Element?

It is not within man's power to define any quality of the elements. A great part of their effects, however, are known. (C. A. 79 v.)

❖

Where the air will not accommodate a flame, no flame can live nor any animal of the earth or air. . . . Where flame does not live no animal that breathes can live. Too much wind kills the flame while the right amount nourishes it. The flame makes a louder noise when air rushes more furiously. (C. A. 270 r.)

❖

Look upon the light and consider its beauty; blink your eyes and look again; that which you saw at first was not, and that which was no longer is. Who remakes it if the maker continuously dies? (F. 49 v.)

❖

Remember when you comment on water to cite first an experiment and then the reason. (H. 90 r.)

The Properties of Water

That water has tenacity and viscosity is clearly shown in small quantities of water whose drops in separating themselves from the rest before falling stretch until the excessive weight of each drop weakens and overcomes the tenacity of the water which supports it, causing it to break and draw back upward. (Lei. 27 r.)

✧

No part of the aquatic element will rise or move away from the common center except through force. No force is lasting. (C. 15 r.)

✧

Water among the four elements ranks second in density and in volubility. It is never at rest until it joins its maritime element where, unmolested by the wind, it becomes stable and reposes with its surface equidistant from the center of the world. It is the sap and substance of all living bodies; no other thing retains in itself its original form; it binds together bodies and enlarges them through growth.

Anything lighter than water can penetrate it only by force; heat makes it rise freely in the air as fine vapor; cold freezes it, stability corrupts it; in other words, warmth moves it, cold freezes it, stillness corrupts it.

It takes up every odor, color and savor, but in its own right it has nothing. It penetrates all porous bodies; no manmade shelter can ward off its fury; and if it could, it would not endure. In its swift course water bears along things heavier than itself. By its own movement or by rebounding it can rise as high as it can sink. As it leaps and falls, it submerges objects lighter than itself. (C. 26 v.)

✧

As the mirror is transmuted into the color of its objects, so water is transmuted into the nature of the place through which it flows. (Ar. 57 r.)

✧

Water is nature's drayman. (K. 2 r.)

✧

Huge rivers flow underneath the earth. (C. A. 160 v.)

✧

When a drop of water falls into a calm sea, the surface of the sea must imperceptibly increase its level. (C. A. 20 r.)

✧

Water tears apart mountains and fills in valleys and would reduce the earth to a perfect sphere if it could. (C. A. 185 v.)

✧

The surface of the sea is equidistant from the center of the earth and forms the deepest surface in the world. The lowest parts of the mountains are found where they join their valleys, and in the extreme depths of these valleys are the rivers which formed them and which reach their ultimate depth in their concourse into the ultimate stream, where they lose their forms and names; and the deepest part of the ultimate stream is the sea where the wandering kindred streams find repose. (A. 56 v.)

✧

The sea is the universal mirror and unique resting place of the wandering waters of the rivers. (C. A. 106 v.)

✧

Water consumes the tall peaks of mountains; it undermines and removes great rocks. It drives the sea over its former banks. First it raises the floor with the earth that it carries along; then it conquers and destroys its high banks. In it is never seen anything permanent that does not soon corrupt its nature. With its streams it penetrates every slope in the valleys, here taking up and here depositing new earth; thus we can say that there are many streams through which all the water of the earth has flowed into the sea and that the sea has returned the water many times. No part of the earth is so high but that water was once at its base, and no depth of the sea is so low but that once it was the base of towering mountains. (Ar. 57 r.)

✧

Among the forces that work harm on man's goods, streams with their powerful and furious inundations appear to me to take first place.

Anyone who tried to set fire above the fury of ruinous streams would seem to me to be lacking in good judgment, for fire comes to an end and dies whenever it lacks nutriment. But against the irreparable inundations of swollen and raging streams no device contrived by man avails; turbulent and tumultous streams tear at and destroy their high banks, rage through the lands under cultivation, ruin houses, uproot tall trees which they carry as booty to the sea, their resting place. Flooding dikes and every other bulwark, they carry away men, plants, beasts, towns, and property.

They carry away light objects and ruin and destroy heavy ones, making of small fissures great ravines, filling deep valleys with their overflow, and rushing ever onward with their harsh, noxious waters. (C. A. 361 v.)

The Effects of the Air

When force creates a motion faster than the resistance of the movement of air, then the air condenses in much the same way as the feathers that are pressed together and compacted by the sleeper's weight; and the thing that presses against the air, finding it resistant, rebounds in the same way as a ball thrown against a wall. (Triv. 6 v.)

✧

I hold that the air appears blue not because blue is its color but because of warm humidity, vaporized into very minute and imperceptible atoms, which attract and are struck by the sun's rays and become luminous under the obscurity of the vast darkness of the region of fire which serves as its covering.

This you will see, as did I, if you climb Monboso. . . . The air above me was dark, and the sun as it struck the mountain was more luminous there than down in the plain. (Lei. 4 r.)

How Water Once Covered the Earth

Since things are much older than writing, it is not surprising that in our days there appears no written record indicating that the sea once covered many lands. Even if some written evidence had appeared, wars, fires, changes in languages and scripts, and floods would have consumed everything from the past. But for us proof enough is that things born in salt water are found on high mountains, far from the sea. (Lei. 31 r.)

Of the Flood and of Mussels

If you say that mussels which today can be seen at such great heights far from the sea in regions of Italy were left there by a flood, I answer that if you believe that such a flood was higher than the highest mountain by seven cubits—as whoever measured it wrote—mussels, which are always found near the seashore, would be found strewn all over the tops of mountains and not scattered through layer after layer at their feet.

And if you say that the mussels were lying cozily on the seashore and that when the water rose to such great heights they left their original places and followed the rising waters up to their highest point, I answer that since a mussel moves no faster than a snail out of water—even somewhat more slowly since it does not swim but supports itself on the sides of the furrow that it makes as it moves through the sand—it may travel from three to four ells in one day. Mussels could not therefore have traveled all the way from the Adriatic Sea to Monferrato in Lombardy, a distance of 250 miles, in forty days, as whoever kept account of the time said.

And if you say that the waves carried them there, I answer that these mussels are forced by their weight to remain on the bottom; and if you will not grant me this, you must at least admit that they would have had to remain on the summit of the highest mountains or in the lakes that are imprisoned in the mountains. . . .

And if you say that the empty shells were borne there by the waves after the mussels died, I answer that the dead are never found very far from the living, and that in these mountains are found only those that were alive, for they are known to have shells that watch and to be in layers where no dead ones are found. Furthermore, a little higher up is a layer where all the dead, their shells separated, were thrown by the waves. Near these points streams fell into the sea from great heights, in much the same way as the Arno which today falls from the Gonfalina not far from Monte Lupo. . . . Farther down was discharged the mud in which lived the mussels whose shells were piled up by stages according to the floodings of the turbid Arno as it poured into the sea and over the years raised its bed and accounted for the distribution of the shells. This is revealed by the cut in the Colle Gonzoli, created by the Arno as it eroded its bed; in it are seen clearly the different layers of shells in bluish mud, together with various things from the sea. . . .

If the mussels had been carried by the turbid flood, they would have been scattered throughout the mud and not distributed by distinct layers as they are still seen today. (Lei. 0 v.)

The Ancient Mediterranean

As the waters are lowered by the run-off of streams, no part of the earth is unveiled that was not once a surface looked upon by the sun. (C. A. 45 v.)

✧

As the River Po in a short time lays dry the Adriatic Sea, in the same way it once laid dry a great part of Lombardy. (Lei. 27 v.)

✧

The Mediterranean, the queen of waters, received the royal Streams of Africa, Asia and Europe which fronted upon it and with their waters reached the slopes of the surrounding mountains that dammed it in. The peaks of the Apennines, like islands in this sea, were surrounded by salt water; and still Africa with its Atlas Mountains did not disclose to the heavens her great plains that stretch for almost three thousand miles, and still Memphis lay on the
44

bed of this sea; and above the plains of Italy, where great flocks of birds now fly, fish used to swim in great schools. (Lei. 10 v.)

Proof That the Earth Is a Star

You must first describe the eye, then show how the twinkling of the stars originates in the eye, why the twinkling of one star is greater than that of another, and how the rays of the stars owe their existence to the eye. (F. 25 v.)

Properties of the Sun

The sun has body, form, motion, radiance, heat, and procreative power, and these things flow from the sun without diminishing it. (C. A. 270 v.)

✧

The motion of the elements originates in the sun. The heat of the universe is generated by the sun. The light and heat of the universe come from the sun, and cold and darkness from the absence of the sun. (Ar. 205 r.)

✧

The numberless images which are reflected by the numberless waves of the sea as the sun's rays strike them are the cause of the continuous and boundless radiancy of the sea's surface. (Ar. 94 v.)

✧

They say that the sun is not warm since it is not the color of fire but is much whiter and brighter. To this I answer that when molten bronze is hottest, it is most like the color of the sun, and when least hot, the color of fire. (F. 34 v.)

✧

The sun does not move. (An. C. V. 25 v.)

✧

The sun has never seen a shadow. (C. A. 300 r.)

Praise of the Sun

If you look upon the stars without their rays (as can be accomplished by looking at them through a tiny hole made with the fine point of a needle and held almost touching the eye), you will see that they are so small that nothing could appear smaller. And in fact their great distance accounts for their apparent smallness; many of them are many times larger than our star—the earth and its water.

Now consider what our star would look like at such a great distance, and then consider how many stars might be placed throughout the length and breadth of the dark space in which these stars are scattered. But I can not refrain from criticizing many of the ancients who said that the sun was no greater than it seemed. Among them was Epicurus. I believe that he based his reasoning on the fact that the light placed in our air is equidistant from the center: whoever sees it in the distance never sees it diminished in magnitude. My arguments concerning its magnitude and force I reserve for the fourth book, but I marvel indeed at the fact that Socrates thought lightly of this body and said that it was like a glowing stone; certainly whoever reprimanded him was in the right.

I wish I might find words to condemn those who see fit to praise the worship of men more than the worship of the sun, for I do not see in the whole universe any body of greater magnitude and power than it. Its light illuminates all the heavenly bodies scattered throughout the universe; all souls derive from it, for all heat that is in animals comes from the soul, and there is no other heat or light in the universe, as I shall show in the fourth book; and certainly those who wished to worship men as gods—Jupiter, Saturn, Mars, and the like—made a very serious mistake in thinking that man, even if he were as big as our earth, would look like the smallest star, which seems like a point in the universe; and further in thinking that men are mortal and crumble and decay in their graves.

La Spera and Marullo, along with many others, praise the sun. (F. 5 r.)

46

The Earth and the Moon

Your whole discussion ought to point to the conclusion that the earth is a star almost like the moon. In that way you will attest the nobility of our world. Your treatise on the magnitude of many stars will give the opinions of other writers. (F. 56 r.)

✧

The earth is not in the middle of the circle of the sun nor in the middle of the world but rather in the middle of its elements, associated and united with them; and if someone stood on the moon when both it and the sun were beneath us, to him the earth with the element of water would have the same appearance and would carry out the same office as the moon to us. (An. C V. 25 v.)

✧

Here you have to prove how the earth serves the moon in the very same way as the moon serves the earth. (Ar. 104 r.)

✧

Either the moon has or it has not its own light. If it has its own light, why does it not shine without the help of the sun? And if it has not its own light, it must be a spherical mirror. The moon does not have its own light but shines only as long as the sun makes it shine; and we see exactly as much of its light as it sees of ours.

Its night receives as much brightness as our waters lend to it as they reflect the image of the sun on it, for in all the waters which they look down upon, the sun and the moon are reflected. The earth and the moon lend each other light. (C. A. 174 v.)

✧

Here you see the sun light the moon, a spherical mirror; as long as the sun lights the moon, the moon shines. (Ar. 28 r.)

✧

The moon is a solid, opaque body; and if it were on the

47

contrary transparent, it would not absorb the light of the sun. (Ar. 9 v.)

✧

Make eyeglasses to magnify the moon. (C. A. 190 r.)

✧

The moon, dense and heavy, dense and heavy, how does it stay there, the moon? (K. 1 r.)

✧

This is a manifest sign that the moon is provided with its own elements—water, air, and fire—and that it sustains itself in and by itself in that space, as does our earth with its elements in this other space. (Lei. 2 r.)

Moon Spots

It is said that moon spots are created by the alternation of thick and thin layers. If this were true, solar rays would penetrate these layers during eclipses; since this effect is not seen, this interpretation is false. (F. 85 r.)

✧

It is also said that vapors in the form of clouds rise up and get between the moon and our eyes; if this were true, these spots would never be stable in position and in form; and if the moon were viewed from different points, then these spots, even if unchanged, would have a different form, as happens in the case of things that are seen from different sides.

Some say that the moon is made up of parts that vary in transparency, as if one part were like alabaster and another like crystal or glass, from which it would follow that when the sun strikes the least transparent parts with its rays, the light would remain on the surface, and thus the thickest part would be illuminated and the transparent part would reveal the shadows of its dark depths; this, they say, would account for the spots. This interpretation has found favor with many philosophers, and especially Aristotle; but it is a false interpretation, for the changing perspectives of the sun and the moon would reveal changes in these
48

spots: now they would seem dark, now bright. . . . During the full moon the sun would light the transparent part, and since no shadows could be created, the moon would not show us its spots. (F. 84 r.)

The Miracle of the Eye

Because the images of objects are distributed throughout the surrounding air, all the images in our hemisphere together with all heavenly bodies enter and pass through the pupil where, penetrating and intersecting each other, they fuse and unite: the images of the moon in the east and of the sun in the west, together with our hemisphere, are fused and united in the pupil.

O wonderful necessity, with perfect logic you compel all effects to be linked directly to their corresponding causes, and in accordance with your ultimate, irrevocable law, all natural phenomena obey you in the most direct manner possible.

Who would believe that such a small space could contain images of the whole universe? O great deeds, what mind can pervade nature such as this? What tongue can unfold such a wonder? None. This directs human reason to the contemplation of the divine. . . .

Here the forms, here the colors, here all the images of the whole universe are fused in one point. O what other point is so marvelous? O marvelous, O stupendous necessity! Your laws compel all effects to participate directly in their causes! Here indeed are miracles! (C. A. 345 v.)

❖

Because the eye is the window of the soul, the soul is always afraid of losing it, with the result that a man when suddenly frightened by a thing moved in front of him protects with his hand, not his heart, the source of life, nor his head, which contains the ruler of the senses, nor his hearing, nor the sense of smell or taste, but immediately the frightened sense; since it is not sufficient for him to

49

close his eyelids, which he presses together as tightly as possible, he quickly turns away in the opposite direction and, still not feeling safe, puts his hand over his eyes and thrusts out the other one as further protection against the thing that he fears. (C. 1 r.)

How the Eye Functions

Every object put in a certain place appears everywhere and in all its details. If the façade of a building or a square or a landscape which is lighted by the sun has opposite it a house on whose front the sun is not shining, and if a tiny round hole is made through the front wall of the shaded house, then all the lighted objects will send their images into the house through the hole and will appear distinctly but inverted on the opposite wall, which would be white. And if similar holes are made at several different places in the same wall, for each the effect will be the same. (C. A. 135 v.)

❖

It is impossible for the images of bodies that pass through holes into a dark place not to reverse themselves. (D. 10 r.)

❖

Everything seems dark when the eye turns from bright sunlight to a place where there is less light . . .

The pupil increases or decreases according to the brightness or dimness of an object; and since some time is required for it to grow larger or smaller, it does not see immediately after leaving light and entering darkness or after leaving darkness and entering light. I once made a mistake in this respect when painting an eye, and that is how I learned the truth. (For. II, 158 v.)

❖

Nature has also arranged for man's eye to close its lids independently in order that nothing may injure it during sleep and unguarded moments. (C. A. 119 v.)

❖

With respect to bodies of equal size and distance, the

brighter one will seem to the eye to be nearer and bigger.
(C. 1 r.)

✧

That luminous body will appear more brilliant which is
surrounded by the more luminous field. (C. 3 r.)

Principles of Anatomy

My representation of the human body will be as illu-
minating to you as if you had before you an actual human
being. . . .

These fifteen complete drawings will show you the cosmography of the microcosmos in the same order that was
used before me by Ptolemy in his cosmography; and in the
same way I shall then divide those members as he divided
the whole into parts, and then I shall state the function of
the parts in every respect, putting before your eyes information about the whole form and strength of man, insofar
as through his parts he is capable of locomotion.

God grant that I may be able to show the nature and
customs of men as I describe their physiques. (An. C. I, 2 r.)

✧

You who would show man's physique with all the aspects of
its articulation, banish such an intention, for the more de-
tailed you make your description, the more you will con-
found the mind of the reader and the more you will becloud
his understanding of the things described. You must use
drawings to explain and to describe. (An. A. 14 v.)

✧

I remind you not to entangle yourself in words unless
you are speaking to the blind; and if you wish to appeal
to a man's ear with words and not to his eye, speak of
concrete or common things and do not embarrass yourself
by trying to force into his ear things that belong to his eye,
for you will be excelled by far by the work of the painter . . .

With what words will you describe this heart without

51

filling a book? . . . O writers, with what words will you describe the whole structure with such perfection as this sketch does? (An. C, II, 1 r.)

✧

Wondrous instrument, devised by the Supreme Master! (An. B 12 r.)

✧

Show the feet with only the bones; then show them with their covering tissues, and make a simple sketch of the nerves; then over the same bones make one of the sinews; and afterwards the veins and arteries together; and finally, a single sketch that contains arteries, veins, nerves, sinews, muscles, and bones. (An. A, 11 r.)

Comparative Anatomy

I have found in the composition of the human body that, in comparison with the composition of other animals, its sensory perception is blunter and coarser, and that it is also made up of fewer ingenious arrangements capable of receiving sensory impressions. . . .

Man differs from the animals only in unnatural ways. He appears to be divine because, where nature stops producing her species, here man begins with the aid of nature to make numberless species from natural things; self-sufficient animals, on the contrary, are not disposed to look for such things since they find them unnecessary. (An. B, 13 v.)

✧

You will then prepare a treatise on the hands or feet of all animals to show what their differences are. (An. C I, 2 r.)

✧

You will show for this comparison the legs of the frog; they show a great similarity to the legs of man with respect to both bones and muscles. Then you will continue with the hind legs of the hare, which are very muscular and have clearly defined muscles, for they are not covered up with fat. (An. C. V 23 r.)

On Dissecting the Dead

O you who seek to understand our organism, do not be contrite because you learn of it through the death of others but rejoice that our Creator set his mind upon such an excellent instrument! (An. II, 5 r.)

✧

And you, man, who consider in this my tiresome work the wondrous works of nature, if you think the destroying of it to be a nefarious thing, then you must consider the taking of a man's life a most nefarious thing; for though man's organism may seem to you to be a marvelous creation, it is nothing in comparison with the soul which dwells in such a mansion; truly it is a divine thing, and you ought therefore to let it dwell in its beloved work and ought not to seek through anger or ill will to destroy it; indeed, he who does not treasure it does not merit it; and because it departs so reluctantly from the body, I firmly believe that its wailing and grieving are not without cause. (An. A 2 r.)

✧

You who say that it is better to see the results of anatomy than to see an anatomical drawing would be right if it were possible to see all the things that are shown in one figure in a good drawing; but in these results you with all your skill will see and gain knowledge of only a few blood-vessels; in contrast I, to get accurate and complete knowledge of the blood-vessels, have dissected more than ten human corpses, cutting up all their other members and removing with the greatest care all the flesh from around them, without spilling any of their blood other than that from the imperceptible bleeding of the capillary veins. Since a single corpse did not last a sufficient time, I had to proceed from corpse to corpse and thus collect complete information; and this I repeated twice to see the differences.

Even if you had a love for such a thing, you would perhaps be prevented by your stomach; if this did not stand in your way, you would perhaps be prevented by the fear of living at night in the company of such quartered and skinless corpses which are frightful to see; if this did not prevent you, perhaps you would lack the ability to draw well, which is necessary for such illustration; if you could draw, you might not have the right perspective; if you had the right perspective, you might not know the method of geometrical proofs and the method of calculating the strength and capabilities of muscles; or you might lack patience and therefore fail to exercise diligence.

Am I endowed with these attributes? The one hundred and twenty books composed by me will render a verdict of yes or no. They have been held back not by greed or negligence but only by time. (An. I, 1 v.)

Physicians

Seek to preserve your health. This you will succeed in doing if you stay away from physicians. Their prescriptions are a kind of alchemy, and on this subject there are as many books as medicines. (An. A 2 r.)

The Art of Painting

The divine element in the art of painting changes the painter's mind into a likeness of the divine mind, giving him the power to evoke the manifold forms of different animals, plants, fruits, regions, and cleft mountains; fearsome and awesome places that terrify their viewers; gentle, peaceful landscapes that delight the eye with their colorful meadows in flower, softly undulating as the gentle wind moves fleetingly over them; streams swollen by heavy rains descending from high mountains, driving before them uprooted plants mixed with rocks, roots, earth and scum, and carrying along with them whatever is in their path of destruction; and the sea as it struggles with the tempest and scuffles with the wind that assails it—as it mounts superb waves that are splintered and converted into foaming froth by the wind which they imprison as they fall. (Lu. 68)

❖

Drawing is of such excellence that it seeks out not only

the works of nature but also countless other works not made by nature. (Lu. 133)

✤

The true, scientific principles of painting . . . are grasped by the mind alone, without recourse to any manual effort. (Lu. 33)

Painting and Nature

If you despise painting you do not love philosophy in nature. If you despise painting, which is only the imitator of the manifest works of nature, then certainly you will despise an invention that considers all qualities of forms philosophically and with subtle deliberation: air and landscapes, plants, animals, herbs and flowers girdled by shadow and light. Truly this science is the legitimate daughter of nature, for painting is born of nature. Or to put it more correctly, let us say that painting is the granddaughter of nature, for all manifest things are born of nature, and among these is painting. We can rightly call painting the granddaughter of nature and the close relative of God. (A. 100 r.)

Painting and the Eye

Painting takes advantage of all ten of the functions of the eye—the perception of darkness, light, body and color, figure and place, distance and nearness, motion and rest. My little work will be pieced together around these functions, with the result that the painter will be reminded of the rule and means by which he ought with his art to imitate all those things which are the work of nature and the ornament of the world. (A. 102 v.)

Painting and Philosophy

Painting embraces surfaces, colors, and forms of everything created by nature; philosophy penetrates these same bodies and considers their characteristic qualities. (Lu. 10)

✤

The painter must be solitary and consider what he sees. He must converse with himself. He must select the quintessence of whatever he sees. He must act as a mirror that changes into as many colors as there are things placed before it; if he does this, he will be as a second Nature.

The painter who copies with his hand and his eye but without reason is like the mirror which mechanically reflects everything placed before it. (C. A. 76 r.)

❖

He should surround himself with others of his ilk; if he finds no companions, he should withdraw with his contemplations, for after all, he will find no more useful company. (C A. 184 v.)

Painting and Aesthetics

The greatest harm is done when the thought is more important than the work. (A. 113 v.)

❖

What moves you, O man, to abandon your own dwelling in the city, to leave your relatives and friends, and to go through mountain and valley in rural regions if not the natural beauty of the world which, all things considered, is enjoyed only through the sense of sight? (Lu. 23)

❖

The painter must have a knowledge of mathematics as it relates to painting, he must give up the company of those who hinder his studies, and he must have an intellect which can follow easily the various directions of the objects placed in front of him and which is removed from all other cares.

If in the contemplation and definition of a particular case a second case intervenes, as happens when the object is seen in a new light, the painter must judge which is the more difficult to define and trace out in detail first, then come back to the definition of the other; and especially he must have a mind like a mirror that changes into as many varied colors as there are colors of the objects before it. (C. A. 184 v.)

❖

We can learn from every journey. Bountiful nature provides for us in such a way that everywhere in the world we find something to imitate. (A. 111 v.)

❖

Do you not know that the soul is harmonious and that harmony is created only at the instant when the proportionality of objects is made visible or audible? (D. 4 v.)

Painting and Anatomy

To show correctly poses and gestures as they affect the limbs of a nude body, the painter must study the anatomy of nerves, bones, muscles, and fibers and know in the case of different movements and forces which nerve or muscle is involved; then he must make only this muscle pronounced and enlarged, and not all the others, as do many who, to appear to be great artists, make their nude figures knotty and graceless, with the result that they look more like a sack of nuts than the exterior of a man, or more like a bunch of radishes than the musculature of a nude body. (I. 79 r.)

The Worth of the Eye

The eye in which the beauty of the universe is mirrored for the observer is of such great worth that whoever consents to its loss deprives himself of the representation of all the works of nature which make the soul that gazes on them content to remain in the human jail . . . but he who loses it leaves this soul in a dark jail with no hope of seeing again the sun, the light of the whole world. . . .

Certainly there is no one who would not rather lose the sense of hearing or of smell than his eyesight: the loss of hearing would mean the loss of all knowledge transmitted by the spoken word, and one would consent to this loss only to avoid losing the beauty of the world which resides in the surface of both the natural and the accidental bodies that are reflected in the human eye. (Lu. 24)

❖

Every part of the pupil possesses the possibility of sight. That vision is not reduced to a point as advocates of the perspective theory hold—that is, that all images of objects come to the eye in the form of a pyramid and are reduced to an angle in which the thing that is seen is judged—will be proven by this experiment. (D. 4 v.)

The Technique of Painting

Try to have the perspective of colors in harmony with respect to every object; in other words, the colors should decrease in intensity as the objects decrease in size at different distances. (An. C VI, 18 r.)

❖

The medium that lies between the eye and the object viewed transmutes the object into its color: as the blue air makes the distant mountain appear blue, so red glass makes whatever the eye sees through it appear red. (Triv. 39 r.)

❖

Shadow is always affected by the color of its objects. (An. C. II, 6 r.)

❖

Where shadow borders on light, notice the parts that are darkest or lightest and those that are most or least indistinct in transitions from shadow to light. (A. 111 v.)

❖

Some outlines ought to be blurred, others distinct. . . . If possible, give clear, distinct outlines to shadows. (An. C II, 6 r.)

❖

Use the same color for trees and the surrounding air unless they are dense or thick-foliaged, such as pines and similar trees. (Ar. 114 r.)

❖

The surface of every body is always affected by the color

of the body that illuminates it and by the color of the air which lies between the eye and the body—that is, by the color of the transparent medium placed between the thing and the eye. (G. 53 v.)

Painting and Poetry

When the poet ceases to depict in words what actually exists in nature, then he is not equal to the painter. If the poet leaves aside such representation and sets down the ornate and persuasive words of his characters, he becomes an orator and is no longer a poet or a painter; if he speaks of the heavens, he becomes an astronomer; and if he speaks of the things of nature or of God, he becomes a philosopher. But if he turns again to the representation of all possible things and tries to emulate the painter, he can satisfy the eye with words as does the painter with paint-brush and color: by producing instantaneous harmony for the eye as music does for the ear. (An. C III, 7 r.)

PART TWO

THE MORALIST AND THE WRITER

Truth and Knowledge

The acquisition of knowledge is always useful to the intellect. The worthless can be rejected, the good retained. Nothing can be either hated or loved until one has had some knowledge of it. (C. A. 226 v.)

❖

Just as iron rusts away without exercise and water grows stagnant or freezes from cold, so without exercise the mind decays. (C. A. 289 v.)

❖

Sad is the pupil who does not surpass his master. (For. III, 66 v.)

❖

As a kingdom divided among itself is destroyed, so a mind divided among different studies is confused and weakened. (Ar. 180 v.)

❖

Our intellect does not set things that happened at various distances in time at their fitting and proper distances; many things that happened many years ago seem near and close to the present while many recent things seem as remote in time as our youth. In the same way, the eye makes distant things lighted by the sun appear near and many things that are near appear distant. (C. A. 29 v.)

❖

Just as eating without appetite is harmful to the health, so study without desire ruins the memory and results in the retention of nothing that is apprehended. (A. 114 r.)

❖

Shun that study of which the resulting work dies along with its creator. (For. III, 55 r.)

Truth and Falsehood

Man has a great capacity for reasoning, but for the most part it is vain and false; the animal has but little, but it is useful and true; a little certainty is better than much falsehood. (F. 96 v.)

✧

Doubtlessly the relation between truth and falsehood is the same as that between light and darkness. Truth is in itself of such excellence that even when it embraces humble and base matters, it exceeds beyond comparison uncertainties and falsehoods spread over grand and eloquent issues. The mind has falsehood as its fifth element, but the truth about things is the best nourishment for the refined intellect, though not for the roving mind.

So vile is falsehood that if it speaks the highest things of God, it mars the grace of His divinity; and so excellent is truth that if it praises the meanest things, it ennobles them.

You who live on dreams take more pleasure in sophistry and in deceptive discussions about grandiose and uncertain things than in reasoning about natural things which, though not so lofty, are certain. (V. U. 12 r.)

✧

The truth works in such a way that a lie tortures lying tongues. (F. 0)

The Mind of Man

The eye and the rays of the sun and the mind are the fastest motion there is. The sun, as soon as it appears in the east, at once speeds to the west with its rays, which are made up of three spiritual potencies: radiancy, heat, and imagery in the form of their cause.

62

The eye as soon as it is opened sees all the stars of our hemisphere.

The mind leaps in an instant from the east to the west, and all other spiritual things are vastly different from it with respect to speed. (C. A. 204 v.)

✧

Every action must be effected through motion.

To know and to will are two human acts. To discern, to judge, and to counsel are also human acts. Our body is beneath heaven and heaven is beneath the spirit. (Triv. 36 v.)

✧

The razor that ran away from the barber to lead an idle life actually rusted away. . . . The same thing happens to minds which give themselves over to idleness instead of to exercise; like the razor they lose their keen edge and the rust of ignorance ruins their form. (C. A. 289 v.)

Natural Law

Contra.—Why did nature not ordain that one animal should not live by virtue of the death of another?

Pro.—Nature is venturesome and takes pleasure in forever creating new living forms, for she knows that these increase her earthly substance. She is willing and able to create more than time can destroy; for this reason she has ordained that some animals must serve as food for others. Nor can this satisfy her desire. She often sends out certain poisonous and pestilential vapors and ever recurring plagues over the great multiplications and congregations of animals, and especially over men, who make great increase since other animals do not feed on them. Once causes are eliminated, their effects will cease.

Contra.—The earth seeks to take its own life, desiring continuous multiplication for the reasons adduced and explained. Effects are often like their causes. Animals illustrate the life of the world.

Pro.—Hope and longing for repatriation and return to

the primal chaos is to man what light is to the butterfly. With a constant joyous longing he awaits the new spring, always the new state, always the new months, the new years; for always it seems to him that the things longed for come too late, and he fails to realize that he is wishing away his own life. This same longing is in the quintessence or spirit of every element; finding itself imprisoned in the form of a soul in the human body, it longs always to return to its emittor. (Ar. 156 v.)

✧

Nature seems here in the case of many animals to be their unnatural mother rather than their natural one, and in the case of other animals to be not only a natural but also a merciful mother. (For. III, 20 v.)

The Wisdom of Nature

The death of some creatures sustains the life of others. In the dead there remains insensate life which when assimilated through the stomachs of living creatures again acquires sensitive and intellectual life. (An. B. 2 v.)

✧

Although the human mind makes various inventions and finds various instruments to answer the same purpose, it will never find inventions more beautiful, simple, and economical than those of nature; in her inventions nothing is missing, nothing superfluous; she does not work with counterweights when adjusting the members to the motion of an animal's body but puts inside the body the soul that shapes it: the soul of the mother who first compounds in her womb the form of man and in due time wakes the soul which is to dwell in the form and which first lay sleeping, protected by the mother soul. The rest of the definition of the soul I leave to the minds of the monks, fathers of the people, who through inspiration know all secrets.

I let stand the Sacred Word, for it is the highest truth. (An. C IV, 10 r.)

✧

Every part tends to unite with the whole to escape imperfection. (C. A. 59 r.)

Body and Soul

The soul can never be corrupted by the corruption of the body but is like the wind which is responsible for the sound of an organ; when a reed is ruined, the wind can no longer produce the right effect. (Triv. 40 v.)

✧

If you wish to understand how the soul dwells in a man's body, observe how his body uses its domicile; if it is disorderly and confused. (C. A. 76 r.)

✧

The soul longs to be with its body, for without the organic instruments of a body it can do or feel nothing. (C. A. 59 r.)

Content and Form

The lover is moved by the beloved as feeling by that which is perceived; their union produces something complete in itself.

Work is the first thing born of their union. If the beloved is vile, the lover becomes vile.

When the unified thing is adapted to its unifier, there follow delight, pleasure, and satisfaction. When the lover is joined to the beloved, there he finds repose. When the burden is set down, there it finds repose. So when a thing is grasped by our intellect. (Triv. 6 r.)

✧

The intellect or the imagination guides and checks the senses, but the things that are imagined move them. (An. B. 2 v.)

Aphorisms

He who does not treasure life does not merit it. (I. 15 r.)

❖

The ambitious who are not satisfied with the gift of life or the beauty of the world are forced to do penance: to them this life is torture, and they are denied the use and beauty of this world. (C. A. 97 v.)

❖

A life well spent is long. (Triv. 35 v.)

❖

He who has his eye fixed on a star does not turn back. (W. 12 282 r.)

❖

Just as a good day's work leads to pleasant sleep, so a life well spent leads to a pleasant death. (Triv. 27 r.)

❖

Acquire something during your youth to provide for your losses during old age. If you intend for your old age to feed on wisdom, so act during your youth that you may not lack food during your old age. (C. A. 111 r.)

❖

If you give yourself over to pleasure, know that you will bring upon yourself suffering and penitence. (Ox. A. 29 r.)

❖

Aristotle in the third book of *Ethics*: Man is worthy of praise and insult only with respect to those things that are in his power to do or not to do. (C. A. 289 v.)

❖

One can have neither greater nor smaller mastery than that over himself. (H. 119 r.)

❖

Ask for advice from those who evidence good self-discipline. (H. 118 v.)

❖

He who does not control his impulse classes himself with beasts. (H. 119 r.)

❖

The passionate mind is ruled by sensuality. (C. A. 358 v.)

❖

A vase broken before it has been fired can be reshaped, but one broken afterwards can not. (Triv. 38 r.)

❖

Small rooms or dwellings direct the mind toward its goal while big ones lead it astray. (A. 96 r.)

❖

Do not undertake things if you see that you will have to suffer in case you do not succeed. (An. B. 21 v.)

❖

You do wrong to praise something and even worse to find fault with it when you do not understand it thoroughly. (C. A. 289 v.)

❖

He who does not punish wrong condones it. (H. 119 v.)

❖

Speaking good of something bad is the same as speaking ill of something good. (For. II, 41 v.)

❖

Criticize a friend in secret and praise him openly. (H. 16 v.)

❖

Spare the traitor from death, for if he practices loyalty, no one will believe him. (H. 118 r.)

❖

The instruments of barratry are the seed of human blasphemy against God. (C. A. 358 v. a)

❖

The goldfinch feeds spurge to its caged young: better to suffer death than to lose their freedom. (H. 63 v.)

❖

Where there is more feeling, there is also more suffering among martyrs. (Triv. 23 v.)

❖

God sells us all our goods at the price of much toil. (W. 12 642 r.)

❖

With virtue is born envy; there would be a body without a shadow sooner than virtue without envy. (Ox. A. 29 v.)

❖

Hands in which ducats and precious stones purl never tire of their service; but such service is for them alone, not for us. (W. 12 700 r.)

❖

Everybody tries to amass capital to give to physicians; they must therefore be rich. (F. 96 v.)

❖

Man has but one obsession: he struggles always to avoid struggling, and life eludes him while he is still hoping to enjoy the goods acquired through his relentless toil. (For. III, 17 v.)

❖

One thing is refused most by those who need it most: advice, which is never heeded by those most in need of it —the ignorant.

One thing draws ever nearer to you who fear it most: misery. The more you flee from it, the more miserable and upset you become. (C. A. 80 v.)

❖

No advice is more sincere than that given from ships in danger. (H. 119 r.)

✧

When I have learned to live, then I believe that I shall also have learned to die. (C. A. 252 r.)

✧

Do not count as riches anything that can be lost. Virtue is the true wealth and reward of its owner. It can not be lost; it does not forsake us, unless life leaves us first. Earthly goods and material riches are always warily held; often their owner, on losing possession of them, is left duped and scorned. (A. 114 v.)

✧

Patience acts against all wrongs in much the same way as clothing against cold; for if you add more clothing as it gets colder, the cold can not harm you. Similarly, you must have more patience in the case of great wrongs; then these wrongs will not injure your mind. (C. A. 117 v.)

✧

Those who possess some worth are treated no differently than I by other men. I have reached this conclusion: It is bad if your enemies are unfriendly and worse if they are your friends. (W. 12 495 v.)

✧

Many traffic in deceits and pretended miracles, deceiving the foolish crowd; if someone shows that he sees through their deceit, they punish him. (F. 5 v.)

Pleasure and Remorse

Here pleasure and remorse are shown as twins because they are never separated from each other. They are shown with their backs toward each other because they are opposites. They are also grafted on the same body because they have the same basis; the basis of pleasure is suffering with remorse, and the basis of remorse is vain, lascivious pleasure. Here a cane is in the vain and powerless right hand; its pricks are poisonous. In Tuscany canes such as this one are used as supports for beds. There people have idle dreams and waste most of their lives. There they waste the valuable morning hours when the mind is sober and calm and the body ready to take on new labors. There people also give themselves over to many vain pleasures; with their minds they imagine impossible things and with their bodies they indulge in those pleasures which often endanger life. (Ox. A. 29 r.)

Tyranny and Freedom

To preserve the principal gift of nature, freedom, I shall find a means of offense and defense against the attacks of ambitious tyrants. I shall speak first of the walled fortress and then of the means by which people can preserve their good and just lord. (Ash. I, 10 r.)

✧

All the animals languish, filling the air with their lamentations. They ruin forests and rend mountains to wrest from them their stores of metals. But what is more perfidious than those who praise heaven after they have rashly injured their fatherland and the human race? (C. A. 382 v.)

Methods of Remaining under Water

A man can not stay under water longer than he can hold his breath. Many men manage to stay under water for some time with special devices. I can stay under water as long as I can go without food, but I shall not publish or divulge my method on account of the base nature of men, who would commit murder on the high seas by breaking through the bottom of ships and sinking them with all the men

70

aboard. Though I teach other methods, they are not dangerous, for above the water, supported by a bottle or a cork, appears the mouth of the tube used for breathing. (Lei. 22 v.)

The Common Man

It seems to me that uncouth men with vulgar manners and limited intelligence do not merit such beautiful tools or such varied contrivances as studious men with extraordinary intelligence. They deserve rather nothing more than a sack in which to receive and excrete food, for they are but foodbags. They have nothing in common with the rest of the human race except their voices and their shapes; in everything else they are like beasts. (An. B 21 v.)

❖

Some men can be classed only as gulpers and squatters—and as makers of dunghills—since they contribute to the world no virtuous acts and since they leave to the world only their great heaps of dung. (For. III, 74 v.)

Time

Among the great things that are found among us nothingness looms large. It resides in time and extends its members into the past and the future. With them it bestrides all works of the past and all works to be, those of nature as well as those of living creatures. Yet it possesses no part of the indivisible present. Nor does it penetrate into the essence of things. (C. A. 398 v.)

❖

The instant is timeless. Time is constituted by the movement of instants, and instants are the bounds of time.

A point has no dimensions. A line is the extension of a point; and points are the bounds of time. (Ar. 176 r.)

❖

A point is not part of a line. The water that you touch

71

in streams is the last of that which goes and the first of that which comes; the same applies to the present time. (Triv. 35 v.)

❖

Men wrongly bewail the flight of time, charging that it passes too swiftly, but they fail to note that they have ample time at their disposal; for a good memory, with which nature has endowed us, makes it possible for everything that happened long ago to appear to us in the present. (C. A. 76 r.)

❖

We have no dearth of ways or means of dividing and measuring our miserable days. These instruments help us to refrain from spending and squandering them foolishly and to do something praiseworthy in order to leave behind some memory of us in the minds of mortals. (C. A. 12 v.)

❖

O sleeper, what is sleep? It is the likeness of death. O why not create such a work that after death you may be the likeness of perfect life and not during your life the likeness of pitiable death through sleep? (C. A. 76 v.)

❖

O time, ravisher of all things! O invidious age! You destroy all things and devour them with the hard teeth of old age—gradually, with slow death.

Helen, looking into the mirror and seeing the withered wrinkles made on her face by age, groans and wonders why she was twice raped. (C. A. 71 r.)

The Fossil Sea-Monster

O powerful and once animate creation of ingenious nature! Since your great strength was of no use to you, you found it necessary to abandon your tranquil life and to obey the laws that God and time imposed on productive nature.

Of no use to you is your jagged, knotty spine with which you furrowed the salty waves that your chest tore furiously apart as you chased your prey.

O how many times the frightened schools of dolphins and giant tuna were seen fleeing before your pitiless rage! With your swift, jagged wings and lashing forked tail you raised on the sea sudden tempests which dashed ships wildly about and sank them; great waves flooded the barren beaches with frightened, floundering fish; having escaped from you, they remained on the beaches left dry by the sea; there in great numbers they fell prey to the neighboring tribes.

O time, consumer of all things, in your continuous circular sweep, give a new and different dwelling place to every life that you have taken away!

O time, swift ravisher of all created things, how many kings, how many peoples have you cut down, and how many changes in states and varied events have you unfolded since the miraculous form of this fish died here! . . .

Now, defeated by time, you lie patiently in this enclosure. Your naked bones stripped clean of flesh, you now support the mountain that towers above you. (Ar. 156 r.)

❖

Everything changes with time. (Ar. 57 r.)

❖

Time in its flight passes secretly and deceives living beings; nothing goes more swiftly than the years; and he who sows virtue reaps renown. (C. A. 71 v.)

The Fable of the Flint and the Steel

The flint, astounded by the attack of the steel, shrieked: "What presumptuousness moves you to punish me this way? Do not beat me; you have mistaken me for someone else; I have never displeased anyone." To this the steel replied: "Be patient and you will see what fruit shall spring from you." At these words the stone, reassured, patiently suffered the beating and saw the wondrous fire with power to work numberless miracles spring forth.

73

This fable is told for the benefit of those who become frightened at the beginning of their studies and then manage through self-discipline to work patiently and continuously until they see the wondrous things that result from their efforts. (C. A. 257 r.)

The Fable of the Pear-Tree

Envying the great quantity of fruit produced by its neighbor the walnut-tree, the pear-tree decided to do the same. It overloaded itself to such an extent that the weight of its fruit broke its limbs and pulled it down to the ground. (C. A. 76 r.)

The Fable of the Nut-Tree

The nut-tree displayed its fruits. Everyone who passed along beneath it cast stones at it. (C. A. 76 r.)

The Fable of the Fig-Tree and the Elm

A fig-tree noticed that a nearby elm bore no fruit and had the audacity to withhold sunlight from its figs. It reproached the elm, saying: "O Elm, are you not ashamed to stand in front of me? Just wait until my children are ripe enough, then you will see where you stand."

Its children later ripened. A squad of soldiers while plucking them tore apart and broke the branches of the fig-tree. Seeing it stripped almost bare of its branches, the elm addressed it, saying: "O Fig-tree, how much better it would have been to remain without figs than because of them to come to such a wretched state!" (C. A. 76 r.)

The Fable of the Thrushes and the Owl

Some thrushes rejoiced on seeing a man take an owl and

rob it of its freedom, binding its feet with strong bonds. The owl, however, through the birdlime snare, caused the thrushes to lose not only their freedom but also their lives.

This fable applies to all towns which rejoice on seeing larger towns lose their freedom, only to fall helplessly before the might of their enemy and lose their freedom and often their lives as well. (C. A. 117 r.)

The Fable of the Rolling Stone

A stone, dissatisfied with its surroundings, started to roll down the street. There it was stepped on, run over, and soiled. . . .

That is what happens to those who wish to give up their solitary and contemplative life to come to dwell in the city among people characterized by boundless evil. (C. A. 175 v.)

The Fable of the Butterfly and the Candle

As the colorful butterfly flew aimlessly through the dark air, it caught sight of a light. Immediately it turned toward the light and, circling it time after time, marveled at its dazzling beauty. Not content merely to observe, the butterfly drew nearer as it was accustomed to do in the case of sweet-smelling flowers. The butterfly flew straight ahead and passed boldly through the light, which burned off the tips of its wings, legs, and other ornaments. Lying at the foot of the light, the amazed butterfly considered what had happened; it could not understand how evil and suffering could possibly have come from anything so beautiful. Finally, having recovered to some degree its lost strength, it undertook another flight. This time it passed through the flame and, burned, fell into the oil that nourished the light. Now the butterfly had only enough life left to consider the cause of its injury. To the light it said: "O accursed light, I thought that in you I had found my happiness! Now in vain I deplore my foolish longing. Through suffering I have learned of your destructive and painful nature."

To this the light replied: "So I deal with those who do not know how to use me to their advantage."

This is related for those who, attracted by wanton desires, like the butterfly rush toward them in ignorance only to learn the truth about them through long association, much to their shame and sorrow. (C. A. 257 r.)

Diverse Fables

Seeing itself marred by the ink's ugly blackness, the paper lodged a complaint; but the ink explained that the words formed by it were responsible for the preservation of the paper. (For. III, 27 r.)

❖

The mirror vaunted itself on having in it the reflection of the queen; when she went away, the mirror was reduced to an abject state. (For. III, 44 v.)

❖

The rivulet carried along so much earth and stone in its bed that it was later forced to change its course. (Ar. 42 v.)

❖

The branch of the nut-tree that is struck and beaten after it has brought its fruit to perfection represents those who are struck in various ways by envy as a result of their illustrious deeds. (G. 88 v.)

Bestiary

Wrath.—Of the bear it is said that when he goes to the house of the bees to rob them of their honey, they continue to attack him to avenge themselves; and since he tries to avenge himself on all those that sting him, he avenges himself on none, with the result that his wrath is converted into rage; throwing himself on the ground and using both hands and feet as weapons, he tries in vain to defend himself. (H. 6 r.)

❖

Treason.—The oyster when the moon is full opens its shell wide; seeing this the crab throws into the shell a pebble or a stick and the oyster, unable to close its shell, is eaten by the crab. (H. 14 v.)

✧

Hypocrisy.—The crocodile lays hold on a man and ruthlessly kills him, then mourns over him with a sorrowful voice and many tears; having finished its wailing, cruelly it devours him.

The hypocrite does the same, showering his face with tears over the slightest incident but showing a tiger's heart underneath; in his heart he rejoices over the ills of others but his face has a doleful look. (H. 17 r.)

✧

Falsehood.—The mole has tiny eyes and always stays under the earth; it lives as long as it remains hidden; but when it comes into the light, it dies immediately for it reveals itself; the same is true of falsehood. (H. 9 v.)

Riddles in the Form of Prophecies

Happy are those who heed the words of the dead.
Read good works and be guided by them. (I. 64 r.)

✧

Money and gold.—There will issue from cavernous caves something which will make all the people of the earth toil and sweat and suffer great sorrow, anxiety, and travail in order to have its aid. (C. A. 145 r.)

✧

Metals.—There will issue from dark, gloomy caves something which will bring great sorrow, danger, and death on the whole human race; to many of those who seek it, it will after much suffering bring delight; but those who do not share in it will die in want and in distress. It will engender unending treason; it will drive unhappy men to com-

77

mit more murders, thefts, and acts of oppression; it will breed suspicion among those who seek it; it will destroy the freedom of free cities; it will take the lives of many; it will sow among men much fraud, deceit, and treason. O monstrous creature, it would be better for men if you returned to hell! On account of you great forests are robbed of their trees and countless animals are robbed of their lives. (C. A. 370 v.)

❖

Man's cruelty.— There will be seen on the earth animals which constantly fight among themselves, inflicting great harm and frequently death on each other. Their enmity will know no bounds; their savage members will fell a great part of the trees in the vast forests of the world; and after they gorge themselves, they will continue to feed on their desire to inflict death and suffering and sorrow and fear and flight on all living creatures. Through their measureless pride they will seek to raise themselves to heaven, but the excessive weight of their members will hold them fast to the earth. Nothing will remain on the earth or under the earth and water that is not pursued, chased down, or destroyed; and it will be chased from country to country. Their bodies will be the grave and passageway of all the living bodies which they have killed.

O world, why do you not open and hurl into the deep clefts of your abysses and caverns and no longer show to heaven such cruel and heartless monsters? (C. A. 370 v.)

❖

Fear of poverty.—Wickedness and fright cause many men to be so terrified that they will waste their prodigious strength in running like lunatics in the belief that they are escaping. (C. A. 37 v.)

❖

Misers.—Many are those who will follow zealously, diligently, and rashly the thing that has always frightened them and never recognize its malignancy. (C. A. 370 r.)

❖

Men will pursue the thing that they fear most: they will

live miserably to avoid being plunged into misery. (I. 64 v.)

❖

Men as they get older become more miserly, whereas they ought to become more generous since their days are numbered. The very ones who are thought to have most experience and judgment seek after things and hoard them most avidly when they have least need of them. (C. A. 370 r.)

❖

Dowries.—Whereas once young girls could defend themselves against lust and rape neither through the watchfulness of relatives nor through the thickness of walls, there will come a time when the fathers and relatives of these girls will be forced to pay a high price to those who wish to sleep with them, even if the girls are rich, noble, and very beautiful. It will seem as though nature should extinguish the human race, for it will be useless to the world and will bring destruction to all created things. (C. A. 370 v.)

❖

Churches and monasteries.—Many there will be who leave behind the work and sorrow and poverty of life and worldly goods and will go to dwell in rich, stately buildings, alleging that this is the means of becoming the friend of God. (C. A. 370 v.) ❖

Sale of Paradise.—Numberless throngs will sell publicly and undisturbed things of the highest worth without the consent of the owner; things which were never theirs nor in their power, and human justice will not intervene. (C. A. 370 v.) ❖

Monks and saints.—Those who have been dead for a thousand years will support many of the living. (I. 66 v.)

❖

Asses.—Constant toil will be repaid with hunger, thirst, suffering, lashings, and pricks. (C. A. 370 r.)

❖

O careless Nature, why are you so unfair toward your

children, showing yourself to some as a loving, devoted mother and to others as a most cruel and heartless step-mother? I see your children given over in slavery to others with no sign of sympathy; and instead of repayment for services rendered, I see them repaid with the worst possible torment. Always they devote their lives to the welfare of their malefactor. (C. A. 145 v.)

Diverse Riddles

Many are they who will skin their own mother and turn her hide inside out: tillers of the soil. (I. 64 r.)

✧

Men will beat mercilessly the thing that gives them life: they will thrash grain. (I. 65 r.)

✧

Men will throw away their own food: they will sow grain. (I. 63 v.)

✧

The bones of the dead in rapid motion will be seen to decide the fortune of their mover: dice. (I. 64 v.)

✧

Wind passed through the skins of animals will make men jump about: bagpipes will make men dance. (I. 65 r.)

The Giant[1]

I am writing this letter to inform you of happenings in the Near East. In the month of June a giant appeared out of the Libyan desert. . . .

His black face was at first sight horrible and terrible to

—————————

[1] A horror story written in the form of a letter addressed to the Florentine merchant and adventurer Benedetto Dei.

look upon, and especially his deep-set fiery eyes behind their dark frightening lashes that made the sky and earth tremble.

Believe me, even the boldest man hastily would have put on wings and taken flight when he rolled his flashing eyes; infernal Lucifer would seem angelical in comparison with him. His turned-up nose had wide nostrils from which there sprouted many coarse bristles; under it was his protruding mouth and on each side his yellow tusks; on the edges of his thick lips grew cat-like whiskers. His instep spanned a man on horseback. . . .

His anger changed to rage and his powerful legs shaking with fury, he began to crush the crowd under his feet and to kick into the air men who fell on each other like hail. And many were they who, dying, brought death to others; and this cruelty lasted until the dust raised by his big feet filled the air and compelled the infernal fury to withdraw.

And we continued our retreat.

O how many vain assaults were made against the devilish fury, for nothing could injure him! O wretched people of no use to you were your impregnable fortresses, the high walls of your cities, your great numbers, your houses and palaces! All you had left were your small burrows and your underground caves; only in the fashion of crabs and crickets and other such animals did you find health and safety! . . .

Certainly in this respect the human race must envy all other species of animals. For truly, though the eagle surpasses the other birds in strength, it does not surpass them in swiftness of flight; martins escape the rapine of the falcon by their speed; and dolphins by swift flight escape the rapine of whales. But flight was of no use to us wretched creatures; with slow tread, this fury outran the fastest runner.

I did not know what to say or what to do. I could see myself swimming head foremost into his great jaws and remaining in the darkness of death, buried in his great belly. (C. A. 96 v. b)

❖

When the savage giant fell as a result of the slipperiness of the ensanguined earth, it seemed that a mountain was falling. The land was shaken, as if by an earthquake, violently enough to frighten infernal Pluto. He lay for some time on the flat ground, stunned by the hard fall, whereupon the people, thinking that he had been struck dead by a bolt of lightning, immediately came back and pulled themselves up his heavy beard. Like ants scurrying back and forth over the trunk of a fallen oak, they began to run one after the other across his huge body, inflicting many wounds. . . .

They held fast to his hair and tried to find hiding places there. They acted like sailors who, preparing for a storm, clamber up the ropes to lower the sails.

The giant regained consciousness. Feeling himself almost covered by the crowd and suffering from their stabs, he suddenly gave forth a roar that seemed like a mighty thunderclap. Then he put his hands to the ground and raised up his hideous face; and as he put one of his hands on his head, he found it full of men that clung to his hairs like the little animals which are supposed to be born of them. As he shook his head, the men flew through the air like hail lashed by the wind; the result was that many of the men were killed by others who were hurled down on them. Then standing up, he trampled them underfoot. . . . (C. A. 311 r.)

The Realm of Venus

From the southern coast of Cilicia is seen the beautiful island of Cyprus, the kingdom of the goddess Venus. There impelled by her beauty, many have wrecked their ships and rigging on the reefs ringed by turbulent waves. Here the beauty of the gentle hills invites the roving sailor to relax in their flowering green from which the playful wind carries soft scents throughout the island and the surrounding sea. O how many ships have foundered there! How many have been dashed against the reefs! Countless ships lay there, broken apart and half-covered by sand, some showing their sterns, some their bows; some keels, others ribs. And it was as if the Last Judgment had resurrected all dead ships, so many were they that covered the whole northern shore. Here the north winds, resounding, make many fearsome noises. (W. 12 591 v.)

To the Viceroy of Syria

This peak is seen over a wide area of the west, lighted by the sun after sunset, for a third of the night. This is the same peak which, during fair weather, was judged to be a comet. In the darkness of the night it seems to us to assume different forms, now broken into two or three parts, now long, now short. This is caused by the clouds which appear on the horizon between one side of the mountain and the sun; they cut off the rays of the sun, and since the light is broken up by clouds of different densities, its radiancy varies. (C. A. 145 v.)

The Survivors

Since I have rejoiced with you many times in my letters over your good fortune, I know now that you as my friend will be as saddened as I over the wretched state in which I find myself. And that is because during these past days we—the other wretched inhabitants of this region and I— have suffered such distress, fright, danger, and harm that we all have reason for envying death. . . .

At first we were assaulted and overwhelmed by the impetuosity and fury of the wind. After that came the avalanches from the snow-covered mountains; these choked up our valleys and claimed a large part of our city. And not content with this, fortune suddenly flooded all the lower part of the city; then came a sudden cloudburst, then a ruinous storm with water, sand, mud and rocks intermixed with roots, briars, and fascicles from various plants. All these things were sent flying through the air and came down upon us. Finally came a conflagration which seemed to be driven not by the winds but by three thousand devils; it burned and laid waste our whole land, and still it has not stopped.

The few of us who survived are left in such confusion and fear that, stupefied, we have all gathered together, men and women, great and small, like goatherds in the ruins of churches; and if certain tribes had not provided us with food, we should have died of hunger.

Now you see what our situation here is; and all these evils are as nothing in comparison with those that are promised us presently. (C. A. 214 v.)

The Flood

Let dark gloomy air be scourged by the rush of diverse winds and framed by continuous rain mixed with hail and carrying now here, now there, vast mazes of mangled plants mixed with the infinite varieties of autumn leaves. All around, there should be ancient trees, uprooted and borne along by the fury of the winds. The mountains, undermined by the flow of their own streams, crumbled and with their ruins dammed up their valleys; these swollen streams then spread out and submerge great regions and their populations. Also you might show gathered on the peaks of numerous mountains many different species of animals, startled and forced at last to entrust themselves to the company of the men, women, and children who had sought refuge there. And on most of the surface of the water that flooded the fields were tables, bedsteads, boats, and various other devices fashioned of necessity and through fear of death; on them were men and women with their children, all moaning and groaning, frightened by the fury of the winds which with awesome might whirled the water round, and with it the bodies of those who had drowned. And there was nothing lighter than water that was not covered by diverse animals which, having agreed on a truce, were now tightly bound together by fear. . . .

You might have seen some groups of men who with weapons in their hands defended the tiny domains left to them against lions and wolves and predatory animals that sought safety there. O what frightful sounds were heard through the dark air, pierced by the fury of thunders and the bolts of lightning which when released rent the air and struck whatever blocked their path! O how many men closed their eyes with their own hands to escape from the loud noises made by the thunder and lightning in the heavens and carried through the murky air by the fury of the rain-drenched winds!

Others, finding that they had to do something more than to close their eyes, covered them with both hands, one over the other, to avoid the sight of the cruel torture that was inflicted on the human race by the wrath of God.

O how they wailed! How many terrified men were hurled from the cliffs! Huge branches of great oaks, laden with men, were borne through the air by the fury of the impetuous winds.

How many boats were capsized! And on all of them, whether intact or broken to pieces, were clinging people who toiled to escape with grievous gestures and movements that announced their horrible deaths. . . . (W. 12 665 v.)

Facetiae

Calling on the authority of Pythagoras, one man tried to prove that he had previously been in this world more than once. When the other man would not let him conclude his argument, he said: "And to prove that I was in the world before, I remember that you were then a miller." The other man, piqued by his words, confirmed that this was true and that he now remembered that the first man had been the ass that used to carry flour for him. (M. 58 v.)

✧

A man was told that he should get out of bed because the sun had already risen. He replied: "If I had to travel as far and do as many things as it, I should have been out of bed by this time; but since I have such a short journey to make, I shall not get up for a while." (For. II, 1 r.)

✧

A painter was asked how it was possible that he painted such beautiful figures of dead things, yet had produced such ugly children.

He answered that he made his pictures by day and his children by night. (M. 58 v.)

✧

The Franciscan friars were accustomed during periods of fasting to eat no meat in their convents; but while traveling, because they lived on alms, they were allowed to eat whatever was placed in front of them. Now it happened that during such a journey two monks of this order arrived at an inn at the same time as a certain petty merchant; the latter, sitting at the same table, saw that on account of the poverty of the inn only one baked pullet was brought to the table; realizing that this would be a meager fare for him, he turned to the monks and said: "If I remember correctly, you do not eat any sort of meat these days." At these words the monks were constrained by their rules to state without further caviling that this was true. The merchant had his way. He ate the baked pullet while the monks did as best they could.

After their meal, the three table-companions again set out together. After they had traveled a little way, the three of them came, on foot—the brothers on account of poverty and the merchant on account of stinginess—to a fairly wide and deep stream. Following the common practice, one of the monks had to carry the merchant on his shoulders. Having given him his wooden shoes for safe-keeping, the monk saddled himself with the merchant.

When the monk came to the middle of the stream, he remembered his rule. Standing still like Saint Christopher, he turned his head toward the one who weighed so heavily on him and said: "Tell me, have you any money?" "Certainly," replied the latter, "Do you think that a merchant like me would travel about any other way?" "Alas!" said the monk, "Our rule forbids us to carry any money." And with that he dropped the merchant into the water.

Realizing that the whole affair was a facetious attempt on

the part of the monk to get even with him for the injury suffered earlier, the merchant blushed from shame and gave a half-hearted laugh. (C. A. 150 v.)

✧

A priest went through his parish on Good Friday sprinkling holy water in the houses as was the custom. Coming into the studio of a painter, he sprinkled some water on some of his paintings. The painter, somewhat angered, turned toward him and asked why he had put water on the paintings.

The priest explained that this was the custom, that it was his duty to do this, that he was doing good, and that whoever does good can expect good and better in return since God promised that every good deed done on earth would be returned a hundredfold from above.

The painter waited until the priest had gone outside, then crossed over to the window and poured a big pail of water on his head. "There," he said, "You are receiving a hundredfold from above for the good that you did with your holy water that ruined half of my paintings." (C. A. 119 r.)

✧ ✧
✧